VICTORIOUS

WINNING THE SPIRITUAL BATTLES AGAINST YOUR
MARRIAGE, FAMILY AND LIFE.

ROB THORPE

First published by All In Marriage, Inc. 12/01/2020

ISBN: 978-0-9833205-8-6 - paperback

ISBN: 978-0-9833205-7-9 - ebook

Printed in the United States of America

For more information, contact:
All In Marriage at marriagesthatmatter@gmail.com
Follow Rob on Twitter at - twitter.com/husbandmentor
Follow All In Marriage at - Facebook.com/allinformarriage
Contact Rob or the Ministry at: marriagesthatmatter@gmail.com

Certain stock imagery © iStockphoto, Bigstockphoto and Clipart.com

Design by Design by: is Chris Paxton / Paxton Creative Services

Because of the dynamic nature of the Internet, any web addresses or links contained in this book may have changed since publication and may no longer be valid

"The tragedy today is that many Christians think they are fighting flesh and blood in their marital and parenting issues, rather than realizing that Satan has an agenda to destroy their home. Whoever controls the family controls the future."

—Tony Evans

CONTENTS

What Was That?

Our wakeup call

MY WIFE AND I WERE deep into a much-needed night's sleep. Our young boys had been asleep for several hours - when out of our oldest son's bedroom came a sound no parent wants to hear, ever....

Screaming–like nothing we had encountered in his three years of little boy activities and adventures–this was different. Not the typical "I don't want to go to bed" protest, or the "I accidentally wet the bed" distress. This was different...way different... scary different.

Matt was screaming.... Frightening, goosebump-causing screaming.

We ran (literally) to his room and threw open the door...and our stereotypical, comfy-casual Christian paradigm would be forever changed.

We immediately noticed two things:

- Matt was sitting up in his bed, but screaming in fear.

- The room felt like a meat locker... ice cold... strangely, eerily cold.

We had been Christians about ten years; attended church and small group faithfully; read our Bibles, led Young Life clubs and Campus Crusade meetings. I had been leading worship at a local church, and we were both involved with the youth there....

But this…this was new; this was different. To be honest, it was a little scary. The kind of scary that makes hair stand up on your arms and on the back of your neck. We both felt that we had come face-to-face with something in the cold darkness that felt creepy…dark…evil…and we had never encountered this before.

First priority? Matt.

I snatched him up and held him close.

Now what?

My mind raced through the Scriptures I had been taught and all the sermons I had ever heard for an answer. What do I do here? Arm hair standing, heart pounding, I uttered the only words that I could come up with ….

"In the name of Jesus", be gone!", I shouted nervously - not knowing what on earth would happen next. But what happened next would forever change our theology.

It was our wake up call.

Matt stopped screaming….instantly. The creepy cold vanished…instantly. The hair on my arms fell back in place and my heart rate normalized. Peace. Instant warmth and peace.

My wife and I looked at each other and said simultaneously… "What was that?"

But we already knew.

We had encountered darkness. Our domain, our home and our three-year-old son…had been targeted by evil.

We talked into the night about our encounter, and I remember my first thought was honestly .. relief (it actually scared the pants off me), but the following thoughts quickly turned to anger.

"Why Matt?" "Why didn't whatever that was pick on someone their own size?" I wondered.

As our mutual blood pressures returned to normal and we settled back down into our bed for the reminder of the night, I remember saying to myself–"This makes me mad–this just got personal!" I boldly proclaimed (to myself)–"I will never let this happen again. I am the father, the husband, the leader and protector of my home… but I have no clue how or why that just happened and what to do to keep it from happening ever again."

The next day, I was reminded of when our small, newlywed home was broken into and robbed while Billie and I were away at church. We didn't have much to steal, but they did take our silver set, my wife's Cameo ring and a diamond ring - both rings were gifts from her side of the family. I remember the feeling of shock when we walked in and realized what had happened. I also remember stupidly picking up a kitchen knife and tactically slinking around the house looking for the intruders - who fortunately weren't there.

But it took some time for us to get over the nauseating feeling that we had been "violated". Evil people had done evil things–to us. "This is supposed to happen to other people".

Solution? Take initiative. Take action. Spend the time and money to buy stronger locks, or an alarm system, or a German Shepherd or something to better protect ourselves from evil and those evil people.

The encounter with Matt scared us. But, thankfully, it also woke us up, and our approach to spiritual life would have to change. We realized, like never before, that we were living in a world at war…and it was not make believe, or just experienced in Jesus' day. We could no longer settle for the "church on Sunday, sing a few songs, give some money, read our Bibles occasionally and pray whenever we felt like we needed it" kind of Christianity. We had been broken into, violated - and that was unacceptable.

We agreed…we needed to be proactive, take initiative - fight - but who were we actually fighting…and how do we win these battles?

The toughest enemy to fight is the one we don't know we have.
Rob Thorpe

In the Beginning...

The history of rulership

IN THE FIRST TWENTY EIGHT verses of Genesis, we are told that God created the heavens and the earth, the planets, stars and moons, and every living thing. He created man and woman and told them to "subdue" the earth and "rule over it". In short, God gave man dominion/rulership over the earth and everything on it.

We find out in the last book of the Bible, that somewhere in that early earth timeframe, some very bad neighbors moved in....

Revelation 12: 7-9 - *Then war broke out in heaven. Michael and his angels fought against the dragon, and the dragon and his angels fought back. But he was not strong enough, and they lost their place in heaven. The great dragon was hurled down—that ancient serpent called the devil, or Satan, who leads the whole world astray. He was hurled to the earth, and his angels with him.*

We find evidence of Satan being on the earth with Adam and Eve just two chapters over in chapter three of Genesis. It is here that we read the all too familiar story of the fall of Adam and Eve. One significant consequence that may not be as obvious from their devastating disobedience was the abdication (surrender) of their rulership on earth to their deceiver.... Satan.

From that point in time on, the earth has been under the rule and reign of Satan and his forces of darkness. Satan is called *"the prince of the power of the air"* (Ephesians 2:2), and the *"god of this world"* (2 Corinthians 4:4). Jesus called him *"the ruler of this world"* (John 12:31). As a result, sin and it's fruit, reigns in the hearts and minds of mankind, and Satan has been allowed to rule over the kingdoms of this world, until Jesus returns to finally re-establish His rule over all–see Revelation 11:15.

Satan spoke of his dominion on earth when he confronted Jesus in the wilderness thousands of years later.

> Luke 4:5-7 - *The devil led him up to a high place and showed him in an instant all the kingdoms of the world. And he said to him, "I will give you all their authority and splendor; it has been given to me, and I can give it to anyone I want to. If you worship me, it will all be yours."*

Satan's mention that "it has been given to me" is a direct reference to Adam and Eve's willing abdication.

Thankfully, Jesus not only died for our sins and to offer us eternal life–he also died and rose again in order to:

"destroy the works of the evil one" I John 3:8

"disarm the spiritual rulers and authorities and shame them publicly by his victory over them on the cross". Colossians 2:15

The crucifixion and resurrection of Christ marked the decisive defeat of Satan. He was judged as a usurper and replaced as the legitimate ruler of this world. Jesus broke the power of Satan over mankind and took back the authority and dominion over the earth. Christ was restored to His proper place of rule, and all things were once again placed "under his feet".

> Ephesians 1:15-23 - *For this reason, because I have heard of your faith in the Lord Jesus and your love toward all the saints,*

I do not cease to give thanks for you, remembering you in my prayers, that the God of our Lord Jesus Christ, the Father of glory, may give you the Spirit of wisdom and of revelation in the knowledge of him, having the eyes of your hearts enlightened, that you may know what is the hope to which he has called you, what are the riches of his glorious inheritance in the saints, and what is the immeasurable greatness of his power toward us who believe, according to the working of his great might that he worked in Christ when he raised him from the dead and seated him at his right hand in the heavenly places, far above all rule and authority and power and dominion, and above every name that is named, not only in this age but also in the one to come. And he put all things under his feet and gave him as head over all things to the church, which is his body, the fullness of him who fills all in all.

But our story doesn't end there. This is the part of the story I either was never taught, or did not fully grasp as a young believer in Christ…

Jesus appeared to his disciples after his resurrection and proclaimed:

Matthew 28:18 - *Then Jesus came to them and said, "All authority in heaven and on earth has been given to me.*

Jesus took it all back! His resurrection defeated sin and death - and he took back His original power and authority to rule and reign over his creation, the earth. He was in charge and was once again able to give rulership to whomever he chose…and guess what happened next?

Jesus gave his disciples, and followers (us included) "all" the power we need to overcome the enemy. (See Luke 10:19). The enemy no longer has power or authority over us as God's children…(unless we abdicate again).

While it is true that Jesus defeated and disarmed Satan at the cross, He knew that we had to continue to live in a world filled his diabolical, evil influence. Thankfully, He also gave us (as His children) His authority and power, as well as spiritual armor and "mighty" weapons with which to overcome the enemy when we encounter him. And do not be deceived, we will encounter him....

> 1 Peter 5:8 - *Be alert and of sober mind. Your enemy the devil prowls around like a roaring lion looking for someone to devour.*

> Ephesians 6:12 - *For we wrestle not against flesh and blood, but against principalities, against powers, against the rulers of the darkness of this world, against spiritual wickedness in high places.*

> 2 Corinthians 10:3-5 - *For though we walk in the flesh, we are not waging war according to the flesh. For the weapons of our warfare are not of the flesh but have divine power to destroy strongholds. We destroy arguments and every lofty opinion raised against the knowledge of God, and take every thought captive to obey Christ*

While judgment has already been pronounced upon him, Satan is still permitted to operate on earth until the time of his final banishment and imprisonment (Revelation 20). As a dethroned monarch, he is still allowed to rule those who accept his authority. He is still the "god of this world" and rules the hearts and minds of those who do not know and follow Christ.

As believers, however, we don't have to yield to Satan's lies, deceit and schemes.

He no longer has authority over us and he can do nothing about our position in Christ.

By putting our faith in the saving work of our Lord Jesus Christ, we have been delivered from the dominion of darkness and brought into the kingdom of God (Colossians 1:12).

But - war has been declared on us...

and we must learn to fight…and fight to win.

> *"Then the dragon was enraged at the woman and went off to wage war against the rest of her offspring—those who keep God's commands and hold fast their testimony about Jesus"* - (Revelation 12:17)

We are locked in a battle. This is not a friendly, gentleman's discussion. It is a life and death conflict between the spiritual hosts of wickedness and those who claim the name of Christ. - Francis A. Schaeffer

CHAPTER ONE

The New Reality...

100,000,000 Bad Guys... Who knew?

❧

I HAD READ THE NEW TESTAMENT stories of Jesus encountering Satan and his minions, and even the disciples after him having to reckon with them as well. But, to be truthful, I never actually thought any of that was more than just good story, or Biblical history - much less, that it pertained to me and my family... today, in the "modern" world.

Why? I really don't have a good answer, so in an effort to avoid personal responsibility, I can easily blame the church for not enlightening and training me. Could they have? Should they have? Absolutely, but I can't place all the blame there. I claimed to be a "Christ-follower", and as such I should have taken His Word more seriously, more literally, more personally.

So, after our bedroom encounter, I set my sights on learning all I could about what we had experienced, where it originated, and how to keep it from happening again. I thought the best place to start would be....well, at the start. Where did this evil come from, and how and why did it come to *our* house?

In the beginning...

What does the Bible say about the devil, Satan and demons? Are they simply metaphors for evil, or representatives of "the dark side"? Since there are many scholarly works devoted to this theme, I will give you my Cliff's Notes version...

Satan is a created being (Colossians 1, Job 1). He's an angel of the category of angels, known as *cherubs* (Ezekiel 28). This is one of the highest classes of angelic beings, and, in fact, he was the highest, most glorious of all created beings. Ezekiel 28 and Isaiah 14 are the two core Old Testament passages providing input into Satan, his fall, and what occurred.

Where did he come from? Like all angelic beings, he was created by God. He was "the model of perfection". He had a heavenly estate. His job was to be the guardian of God's glory – Ezekiel 28. He had more power than anyone, in all the universe, except God, and he was more beautiful than anything, or anyone, but God. The nature of his sin was pride, 1 Timothy 3:6 tells us, as does Isaiah 14:13.

The Satan of Scripture is not a little fella in a red costume. He was the most intelligent, the highest, most beautiful, awesome being in the universe that God had created to that point. But then, like many intelligent, beautiful people do... he became full of himself. He wasn't satisfied with all that he had. He wanted to be God. In Isaiah 14, he made these five statements:

He said, "I will ascend to Heaven." He wanted to occupy the abode of God. He wanted equal recognition with God.

He said, "I will raise my throne above the stars," and the stars, in context here, are the other angels. He wanted to have the top spot.

He said, "I will sit on the mount of the assembly." And the mount of assembly, in the context here, is where God ruled. He was saying, "I want God's rulership position."

He said, "I will ascend above the heights of the clouds." And the clouds indicate the glory of God. He wanted the glory of God. And we know what God says: "I am the Lord. That is My name. I will not give My glory to another." (Isaiah 42:8)

He said, "I will make myself like the Most High." And that's been his strategy ever since. And, in the Garden of Eden, he deceived Eve into believing she too could, "be like God."

At the heart of sin ever since is the same prideful desire for independence, and our inner voice saying, " I want to be like God. I want to be the "god" of my life, the center of attention and praise. I want life to be about me - my dreams, my agenda, my fulfillment and happiness". That was at the heart of Satan's fall.

Isaiah 14:12-15 - *How you have fallen from heaven, morning star, son of the dawn! You have been cast down to the earth, you who once laid low the nations! You said in your heart, "I will ascend to the heavens; I will raise my throne above the stars of God; I will sit enthroned on the mount of assembly, on the utmost heights of Mount Zaphon. I will ascend above the tops of the clouds; I will make myself like the Most High.*

Ezekiel 28:13-17 - *You were in Eden, the garden of God; every precious stone adorned you: carnelian, chrysolite and emerald, topaz, onyx and jasper, lapis lazuli, turquoise and beryl. Your settings and mountings were made of gold; on the day you were created they were prepared. You were anointed as a guardian cherub, for so I ordained you. You were on the holy mount of God; you walked among the fiery stones. You were blameless in your ways from the day you were created till wickedness was found in you. Through your widespread trade you were filled with violence, and you sinned. So I drove you in disgrace from the mount of God, and I expelled you, guardian cherub, from among the fiery stones. Your heart became proud on account of*

*your beauty, and you corrupted your wisdom because of your
splendor. So I threw you to the earth;*

Revelation 12: 7-9 - *Then war broke out in heaven. Michael and
his angels fought against the dragon, and the dragon and his
angels fought back. But he was not strong enough, and they lost
their place in heaven. The great dragon was hurled down—that
ancient serpent called the devil, or Satan, who leads the whole
world astray. He was hurled to the earth, and his angels with
him.*

When Scripture speaks of Satan, it's not some small, passing comment, or a figure of speech, or a metaphor for evil. He is a fallen, powerful angel, who led a rebellion of one third of the angels of Heaven, and they now seek to "*kill, steal and destroy*" (John 10) humanity and especially those of us who are God's children - "*Then the dragon was enraged at the woman and went off to wage war against the rest of her offspring—those who keep God's commands and hold fast their testimony about Jesus*" - Revelation 12:17.

War has been declared….

Did you catch that? Where had this truth been hiding in my decade of listening to sermons and reading God's Word?…let's read that again….

*"Then the dragon (Satan) was enraged at the woman and went
off **to wage war** against the rest of her offspring—those who
keep God's commands and hold fast their testimony about Jesus"*

War has been declared. Satan, the fallen arch-enemy of God, has declared war on God's children, "*those who keep God's commands and hold fast their testimony about Jesus*". That's me…and that's you–if you also claim to be His follower.

Okay, so Satan got mad and declared war on Christians…so what? How does that affect me and my world today?

Before you start to think Satan is a lone ranger, acting solo in a one-man war, may I remind you–He's not acting alone.

> Matthew 25:41 - *Then He will also say to those on His left, 'Depart from Me, accursed ones, into the eternal fire which has been prepared for the devil and his angels;*

> Revelation 12:7-9 - *And there was war in heaven, Michael and his angels waging war with the dragon. The dragon and his angels waged war, and they were not strong enough, and there was no longer a place found for them in heaven. And the great dragon was thrown down, the serpent of old who is called the devil and Satan, who deceives the whole world; he was thrown down to the earth, and his angels were thrown down with him.*

> Revelation 12:4 - *And his tail swept away a third of the stars of heaven and threw them to the earth. And the dragon stood before the woman who was about to give birth, so that when she gave birth he might devour her child.*

How many angels are there? No one really knows. We would probably surmise though that there are a bunch. We see them throughout Scripture as messengers, worshippers, warriors, as well as "ministering spirits" to the millions of people who call themselves God's children. Revelation 5:11 tells us more - *Then I looked and heard the voice of many angels, numbering thousands upon thousands, and ten thousand times ten thousand. They encircled the throne and the living creatures and the elders.*

(math: $10,000 \times 10,000 = 100,000,000$). No one knows how many million…

So, let's say that one hundred million is a good estimate of the angels left in heaven after one-third rebelled, then approximately 50,000,000, were swept out of heaven and *"thrown down to earth"* by aligning themselves with Satan - that is indeed significant.

In case we forget (and I obviously did), we live on that same earth. So, the Bible tells us that Satan has declared war on all Christians and has at least 50 million soldiers at his command in order to wage said war. The picture was becoming much clearer to me.

There are so many angels in fact, (those in heaven and on the earth) that they operate much like our military. They have positions, they have rank, they have varying degrees of responsibility, position, oversight, power and authority.

The apostle Paul tells us that we primarily encounter four distinct categories or ranks of satanic forces. Ephesians 6:12 *"For we wrestle not against flesh and blood, but against principalities, against powers, against the rulers of the darkness of this world, against spiritual wickedness in high places."*

The implications in this passage cannot go unnoticed:

1. We (Christians) *wrestle* - do you ever feel that you are being opposed, oppressed, harassed, tempted, accused, lied to, etc.? Whether we acknowledge it or not - we are wrestling - we are in a war. The Greek word used here for "wrestle" implies "hand-to-hand combat".

2. We don't wrestle against *"flesh and blood"*. The true enemy of our soul is not our spouse, our kids, our boss, or job or neighbor or government. Our enemy can, and does, use those people sometimes to influence us - but they are never the "real" enemy.

3. Words like "powers", "darkness" and "wickedness" should evoke a desire in us to discover who and what we are dealing with (warring with) and how to win this war.

4. The most important question I asked myself at this point, is what I will ask you…. "Are you wrestling?" Wrestling typically involves two combatants battling against each other with the intent to conquer the other. Someone will win and the other will lose. There is no truce,

or treaty. In fact - there is no 2nd place - just the loser. So, if you're not winning, you are losing.

In my case, I didn't even recognize the fact that I was in a war and that there was a need, and a mandate, to wrestle....and to win. How can you wage war if you don't even know (or acknowledge) there is a war going on? An effective tactic by our enemy by the way...

Over the decade I had been a believer at that point, I had witnessed firsthand fellow believers, some much older in the faith than I, who had fallen to temptation, adultery, addiction, divorce, depression and even suicide. I wondered how so many could have believed in Jesus, gone to church and read their Bibles, and yet - ended up so damaged. I began to realize - they didn't know how to wrestle and may not have known at all (like me) that there was a brutal, to-the-death, war waging against them.

My friend - the war is real. The enemy is formidable and relentless. His mission is to "kill, steal and destroy" (John 10:10) you and everyone and everything you hold dear. He does not sleep, or take lunch breaks, or go on vacation. He is working 24/7/365 to fulfill his mission.

I can't imagine that we would walk through the war-ravaged deserts of Afghanistan or Iraq today without first strapping on our bulletproof vest, over which we would sling dozens of rounds of ammunition, buckle our helmet and grab as many weapons as we could effectively carry. Can you imagine heading into the desert in your underwear and sandals?

Sadly - I believe most Christians do just that, and then wonder why they and their loved ones become victims of war.

So, who or what are we up against?

Satan is powerful, but he is a defeated foe.
For the Christian, he is only as strong as the power
we permit him to have in our lives.
Randy Smith

CHAPTER TWO

The Dark Side…

Rethinking Cherubs and Harps

❧

YOU AND I WERE RAISED to believe in good guys and bad guys; heroes and villains; good versus evil…and that good always triumphs over evil. Something in us rises up when we watch Star Wars, Lord of the Rings, Braveheart, Gladiator, Superman, Captain America and the thousands of other movies, books and shows, even cartoons, where the good guys finally win and the bad guys are vanquished. As far back as Snow White, Cinderella, Robin Hood, Popeye, Bonanza, Happy Days, John Wayne - you name it - we have been raised to cheer for the good guys, for the heroes, and to see good win the day.

It's as if there is something inside us, part of our DNA, that acknowledges good and evil and wants good to win. Has God purposefully placed this in our souls to prepare us for the spiritual reality playing out all around us? Could it be that He has been speaking to us all along; warning us, teaching us that we were born into a world at war - where there truly are good guys and bad guys, a Force and a Dark Side, armies, heroes and villains?

Hard to believe, right? I admit, it is hard to wrap our "enlightened", 21st century minds around such things. According to a 2016 Associated Press-AOL poll, and more recent polls by Fox News and CBS, over 80% of Americans believe in the existence of angels.

9

My point is this–if people believe in the existence of angels…nice angels, sweet angels, guardian angels, harp-playing, singing, angels…do they also acknowledge the existence of "bad" or "evil" angels (demons)? As we saw in the previous chapter, the Bible tells us that millions of angels rebelled against God and were booted out of heaven and cast down to earth. These are not the pudgy, harp-playing cherubs we see depicted in old paintings, greeting cards, statues and the like. These are evil warriors, with a mission to destroy everyone they can…especially those who believe in Jesus and follow Him.

These angels are the ones seeking to torment my three-year-old son, destroy my marriage, tempt me into numerous sins and utterly ruin my Christian ministry, witness and legacy.

But, can we really believe in things we can't see?

We would all agree that we benefit greatly from many unseen things in our world… We breathe oxygen; we stay on the earth by gravity and we reap the benefits of electricity daily. Invisible sound waves allow us to enjoy music and communicate with others, while wavelengths of reflected light allow us to experience our world in a dazzling array of color. There are also villains in this unseen world–like viruses, bacteria, ultraviolet light and carbon monoxide. We have no problem believing in an unseen, natural world–because we see the effects (positive and negative) of that world every day.

The Bible is very clear that there is also an unseen world in the spiritual (or supernatural) realm. As we will discover, we see the positive and negative effects of this world in our lives as well. We need to acknowledge this world if we are to understand and be victorious in spiritual warfare.

I find the following story quite enlightening…and funny:

> Numbers 22: 21-35 - *Balaam got up in the morning, saddled his donkey and went with the Moabite officials. But God was very angry when he went, and the angel of the Lord stood in the road to oppose him. Balaam was riding on his donkey, and his*

two servants were with him. When the donkey saw the angel of the Lord standing in the road with a drawn sword in his hand, it turned off the road into a field. Balaam beat it to get it back on the road.

Then the angel of the Lord stood in a narrow path through the vineyards, with walls on both sides. When the donkey saw the angel of the Lord, it pressed close to the wall, crushing Balaam's foot against it. So he beat the donkey again.

Then the angel of the Lord moved on ahead and stood in a narrow place where there was no room to turn, either to the right or to the left. When the donkey saw the angel of the Lord, it lay down under Balaam, and he was angry and beat it with his staff. Then the Lord opened the donkey's mouth, and it said to Balaam, "What have I done to you to make you beat me these three times?" Balaam answered the donkey, "You have made a fool of me! If only I had a sword in my hand, I would kill you right now."

The donkey said to Balaam, "Am I not your own donkey, which you have always ridden, to this day? Have I been in the habit of doing this to you?" "No," he said. Then the Lord opened Balaam's eyes, and he saw the angel of the Lord standing in the road with his sword drawn. So he bowed low and fell facedown. The angel of the Lord asked him, "Why have you beaten your donkey these three times? I have come here to oppose you because your path is a reckless one before me. The donkey saw me and turned away from me these three times.

It took a donkey to enlighten Balaam to the unseen reality right in front of him.

The king of Aram was at war with Israel. Every time he moved his troops to mass a surprise assault on Israel's troops, the prophet Elisha warned the king of Israel by revealing where the enemy troops were located. The infuriated king then sent "a strong force" of men, chariots and horses by night to the city of Dothan to capture Elisha.

Elisha's servant freaked out when he saw a huge army surrounding their city the next morning and feared for their lives. Elisha calmly asked God to show his servant why there was no need to fear; there was something very real, very powerful, the servant had not yet been able to see…

> 2 Kings 6:15-17 - *When the servant of the man of God got up and went out early the next morning, an army with horses and chariots had surrounded the city. "Oh no, my lord! What shall we do?" the servant asked. "Don't be afraid," the prophet answered. "Those who are with us are more than those who are with them." And Elisha prayed, "Open his eyes, Lord, so that he may see." Then the Lord opened the servant's eyes, and he looked and saw the hills full of horses and chariots of fire all around Elisha.*

Daniel (like us) must have wondered why God had not answered his prayers for over three weeks…until an angel appeared to tell him what had occurred in the unseen world…

> Daniel 10: 12-14 - *"Do not be afraid, Daniel. Since the first day that you set your mind to gain understanding and to humble yourself before your God, your words were heard, and I have come in response to them. But the prince of the Persian kingdom resisted me twenty-one days. Then Michael, one of the chief princes, came to help me, because I was detained there with the king of Persia. Now I have come to explain to you what will*

happen to your people in the future, for the vision concerns a time yet to come.

Evidently, a very high ranking principality (remember our discussion of ranks in Chapter 1) over the Persian kingdom fought with (resisted) this angel for three weeks, so that he could not deliver the answer to Daniel's prayer until an even higher ranking angel (Michael) came to help him get through.

Doesn't that honestly sound like a movie script for Hollywood? If we're honest, we find that kind of discussion in Scripture hard to believe, or at least wrap our mind around. The Bible is very upfront though when speaking about angels, Satan, demons and such:

> Psalm 103:21 - *Praise the Lord, all his heavenly hosts, you his servants who do his will.*

> Psalm 148:2 - *Praise him, all his angels; praise him, all his heavenly hosts.*

> Matthew 4:11 - *Then the devil left him, and angels came and attended him.*

> Matthew 26:53 - *Do you think I cannot call on my Father, and he will at once put at my disposal more than twelve legions of angels?*

> Luke 15:10 - *In the same way, I tell you, there is rejoicing in the presence of the angels of God over one sinner who repents."*

> Hebrews 1:14 - *Are angels not all ministering spirits sent out to serve for the sake of those who are to inherit salvation?*

In the Gospels, Jesus dealt with demons and people affected by them nearly every day. He was tempted for forty days in the wilderness by Satan himself and then ministered to by heavenly angels (Matthew 4). Jesus was not only well acquainted with angels and demons, one of the primary reasons he came to earth was to *"destroy the works of the evil one"* (1 John 3:8) - more on that later.

So, if heavenly (good) angels are real, and earthly, hell-bound (evil) angels are real…we need to re-think how they might influence our lives, our marriages and our homes.

A great place to begin would be to examine what we are up against and what they are capable of.

First – They are beings, not just concepts–not some cosmic evil as explained away by many as simply the "opposite of good".

> Jesus was not talking to Himself when He rebuked evil spirits and was tempted by Satan in the wilderness. Matthew 4:1-10; 17:18.

> Satan and his angels can *talk* and even *shout*. Matthew 12:43, 44; Mark 1:23, 24, 26; 3:11; 5:12; 8:31; 9:26; 12:43-45; Luke 4:41; Acts 8:7, 19:15

> They have a *memory* and *know Scripture*. Genesis 2, Matthew 4:6

> They walk *"to and fro in the earth"* and *seek rest.* Job 1:7; 2:2; Ezekiel 28:14; Matthew 12:43, 44

> They have *intelligence.* Ezekiel 28:3, 12

> Know their *time is short.* Revelation 12:12

> They *recognize who the saved are.* Acts 16:16, 17

> They *testify to the divinity* of Jesus Christ. Matthew 8:29; Mark 1:23, 24, 34; 3:11; 5:7; Luke 4:41; 8:28; Acts 19:15

> They are *aware* of their destiny. Mark 5:7; Luke 8:31

They know they have been *defeated* by Jesus on the cross. Colossians. 2:15

Satan and his forces have substantial but limited power

They are *subject to God*. Luke 8:31, 32; James 2:19

They *have power* (2 Thessalonians 2:9; Revelation 2:10), but their power is limited: Job 1:12; 2:6; Mark 1:34; 5:12, 13; 1 Corinthians 10:13-17).

They are *not omniscient* (know your thoughts, know everything) but they are knowledgeable of God's Word, and His followers' doings in the earth.

They are *not omnipresent* (everywhere). Luke 22:3; John 13:27

They are not *omnipotent* (all powerful)

They *know who Jesus is*, fear Him, and they are aware of their destiny. Matthew 8:29; Mark 1:23, 24, 34; 3:11; 5:7, Luke 4:34, 41; 8:28, 31; Acts 19:15; James 2:19

They are *subject to those who believe*. Luke 10:17, 19, 20; Romans 16:20; Ephesians 2:6, Colossians 2:12-15; 1 John 2:13, 14; 4:4; 5:18; Revelation 12:11

Two primary takeaways from this list are: (grab your highlighter…)

1. They are not omniscient

2. They are subject to those who believe in Christ

Since they do not have the power to know our thoughts (omniscient), you must remember to always address them the way Jesus did - **out loud**. You cannot defeat an assault from the enemy by thinking or praying silently....they cannot hear you. We must address them verbally and with the authority we have been given by Jesus. More on that just ahead...

Since they know who believers are, they also know they are subject to the demands of those believers. Like Jesus, like the twelve, and like the rest of his disciples - evil spirits are subject to us but only if we know about, and utilize, the weapons given to us as His children. You guessed it..... there will be more on that up ahead also...

Finally....They are not kidding. The Bible calls Satan (and his armies) our adversary (opponent, enemy). 1 Peter 5:8 *"Be sober, be vigilant; because your adversary the devil walks about like a roaring lion, seeking whom he may devour."*

We have grown accustomed to opponents/adversaries being "the other team" - think college or pro football, or the other contestants on The Voice or Dancing with the Stars. This viewpoint couldn't be farther from the truth. Did you notice the term *"devour"* in the previous verse? *Devour(Gr) = kill and eat - destroy - consume - swallow down.*

Folks, this is not a make believe war. This is no friendly competition, or game.

Everyone doesn't get a participation trophy and then go home. This is literally life and death. There are no peace talks, no treaties, no truces.....this is all out war.

John told us in no uncertain terms - *"The thief comes only to steal, kill and destroy"* John 10:10.

I used to think of my new life in Christ as a life lived out on a Christian cruise ship, sailing through life on my way to heaven. I got my ticket after accepting Jesus as my Lord and Savior, and now life would be filled with Bible studies, worship venues, small group meetings, potluck meals, listening to great sermons and guest speakers, and enjoying wonderful fellowship with friends...until one day...we would dock at the pearly gates, and live happily-ever-after.

What I finally realized is that after accepting Jesus as my Lord and Savior, I was given a uniform, weapons, ammunition, a field guide, a walkie-talkie and a commission....and.... I had landed on an enemy beachhead, fraught with landmines, mortar fire, enemy snipers, and dangers around every corner.

Here is a partial list of war terms that finally arrested my attention -

· wage war / weapons / fight / power / strongholds - 2 Corinthians 10:3-4

· wrestle / struggle / forces / evil - Ephesians 6:12

· fight / battle - 1 Timothy 1:18

· authority / power / enemy - Luke 10:17-20

· power / evil - 1 John 5:19

· armor / schemes /struggle / rulers / authorities / powers / forces / evil / breastplate / shield / flaming arrows / helmet / sword - Ephesians 6:10-18

These are God's words, inspired by the Holy Spirit, that speak very clearly of conflict and war, not of simply attending church, singing and learning new Christian principles to live by. While the latter are vital to the Christian life, the enemy has done a magnificent job of convincing a large percentage of God's people that there is no war, no diabolical enemy and that these words of God don't really apply to us today.

I pray that this book will serve as a wakeup call to open your eyes to the truth...

For our struggle is not against flesh and blood, but against the rulers, against the authorities, against the powers of this dark world and against the spiritual forces of evil in the heavenly realms...Ephesians 6....

is every bit as true today as...

*For God so loved the world that He gave His only begotten son…..*John 3:16

The sooner we recognize it for what it is, the sooner we can suit up and go to battle against the real enemy of our marriage, our family and our life.

Life is war.
That's not all it is.
But it is always that...But most people do not believe this in their hearts.
Most people show by their priorities
and their casual approach to spiritual things that they believe
we are in peacetime, not wartime...
John Piper

CHAPTER THREE

Chalk Talk

Time to Empty the Sidelines

⌘

We would all rather be on a Christian cruise ship than a battleship. We prefer to attend worship services, Bible study classes, small groups and seminars with friends rather than confront a diabolical enemy in prayer, fasting and ministry.... and sadly, many Bible-believing Christians live lives of anxiety, depression, fear and defeat as a result. They describe their marriages as "okay", and tell their friends everything is "fine" when asked about their life. Nowhere in my Bible does God promise an "okay" marriage and a life that is "fine". What He promises is actually quite the opposite.

The thief comes only in order to steal and kill and destroy. I came that they may have and enjoy life, and have it in abundance [to the full, till it overflows]. John 10:10

I have told you these things so that my joy may be in you, and that your joy may be full. John 15:11

And God is able to bless you abundantly, so that in all things at all times, having all that you need, you will abound in every good work. 2 Corinthians 9:8

God promised His people (Israel) a land "flowing with milk and honey", a land of peace and prosperity - but you may recall there were giant people, hostile kings and large armies for them to face before they could occupy and experience this promised land. Similarly, we (Christ followers) are told we can enjoy a life of abundance and complete joy - but we need to also realize that we share a world with a relentless enemy who is hell-bent on keeping us from it. That is why we are also told we will face trials/hardships. (John 16:33 and James 1:2)

Football was one of many sports I played growing up. I vividly recall how my coaches would call us together daily during the season as we prepared for our next opponent. We would sit in our sweaty locker room (think teenage boy sport socks) around a giant chalkboard (no dry erase boards back in those days) while coach ranted on for what seemed like hours. He would describe our opponents' strengths and weaknesses, their favorite offensive and defensive schemes, and their most successful plays and players. With that, he would also go into great detail regarding how we were going to thwart their schemes with some newly developed plays of our own. If we could remember and execute the strategies we had discussed all week in our "chalk talks" - we were confident of victory.

How did our coaches know the schemes and plays of our upcoming opponents? They scouted them at earlier games. Coaches were sent to those games to take film, make notes and document those strengths and weaknesses, those successful plays and players, and bring back this espionage from which to devise our own strategies and counter attacks. We didn't always win (although I did play for two state championship teams), but we won the great majority of our games. Chalk talks worked.

Where are the chalk talks in the church today that prepare us for the most diabolical opponent we will ever face? This opponent is not simply trying to defeat us and get a trophy, he is bent on utterly destroying us and everyone we love. (See John 10:10) While some churches no doubt teach and preach on winning the spiritual battles raging around us, the great majority sadly do not. Why?

> Do they not believe there is a real war going on or a real enemy bent on our destruction?

Are they focused on other, "more important" ministries?

Are they fearful their congregations will begin looking for a "demon under every bush" and turn radical in their approach to Christian living?

Do they believe that dealing with demons was for "then" and not relevant in our modern, scientific age?

Whatever the reason, every time I have taught on spiritual warfare the response I receive is - "where has this been?" or "why haven't I learned this before?". I really don't have a good answer for these people - most of whom have grown up in the church. I do know our enemy does not want us know his schemes and how to defeat them.

So, consider this book your chalk talk.

But remember - chalk talks mean nothing if all you do is stay in the locker room learning more. For several years, there has been a major emphasis in the American church to "equip" believers, and I am all for equipping. Problem is, far too many believers keep putting on more and more equipment, and never get out on the playing field. Going to classes and seminars is a great thing, but there is a time to roll up your sleeves, tighten your chin strap, and get in the game....and that time is now.

The apostle Paul wrote, "*the weapons of our warfare are mighty, to the pulling down of strongholds*" 2 Corinthians 10:4. He also wrote, "*we wrestle not against flesh and blood, but against principalities, powers and spiritual wickedness in high places*" Ephesians 6:12

John wrote, *The reason the Son of God appeared was to destroy the works of the devil.* I John 3:8

Jesus said, "*I did not come to bring peace, but a sword*" Matthew 10:34

Jesus said he would "*build his church and the gates (forces) of hell would not prevail against it*" Matthew 16:18.

Where is the teaching on this warfare and wrestling? What is the modern church doing to kick down (defeat) the gates (forces) of hell? What are you and I doing to free the people we love from the strongholds of fear, anxiety, addiction, depression, guilt, shame and failure? Are we supposed to medicate it all away or depend solely on our church leaders and counselors to help them spiritually?

Jesus wasn't using a metaphor in declaring that the gates of hell would not be able to stand against His people, the church. Early believers healed the sick and cast out demons regularly as they preached the good news of the kingdom. Their commission from Jesus was clear:

As you go, proclaim this message: 'The kingdom of heaven has come near.' Heal the sick, raise the dead, cleanse those who have leprosy, drive out demons. Freely you have received; freely give. Matthew 10:7-9

When Jesus had called the twelve together, he gave them power and authority to drive out all demons and to cure diseases, and he sent them out to proclaim the kingdom of God and to heal the sick. Luke 9:1-2

The seventy-two returned with joy and said, "Lord, even the demons submit to us in your name." He replied, "I saw Satan fall like lightning from heaven. I have given you authority to trample on snakes and scorpions and to overcome all the power of the enemy; nothing will harm you. However, do not rejoice that the spirits submit to you, but rejoice that your names are written in heaven. Luke 10:17-20

Was that for then, but now we live in more civilized society?

Satan and his minions have not gone away, they have not lost sight of their mission or decreased their hatred of those who follow Christ. We don't have to look far in the church or the world around us to see the devastation they are causing in our marriages, our children, in our city streets and our country's moral foundation.

Our late night bedroom encounter was our wakeup call. What will it take to wake you up? What will it take to wake the church up?

Get equipped; stay equipped; but decide it is time to go on the offensive. We need to get on the field, get our elbows and knees bloody, and twist an ankle or two for the sake of kicking down the forces of hell that assault our lives and the lives of those we love.

So, where do we start?

Glad you asked.

No church group that knows spiritual warfare has wiener roasts or even passion plays. There is a real warfare. I have said before that we are an arrogant, self-styled bunch of believers. We "believe" to the point of inconvenience - and then quit.

Leonard Ravenhill

CHAPTER FOUR

A New Perspective

God's view of you

⌘

BEFORE WE DIVE DEEPER INTO spiritual warfare it is crucial that we are grounded in the truth of God's Word regarding who we are as believers, children and heirs. Without this essential truth deep in our hearts (and heads), we will consistently lose the battles.

Most of us have heard and hopefully accepted the fact that we are new creations in Christ; saved by His grace; given eternal life through His sacrifice on Calvary; and able to spend eternity in His presence because of His great love, sacrifice and resurrection from the dead.

As believers, followers, Christians, we have been given some amazing gifts from our Father:

[ ] **Forgiveness of our past, present and future sins**

He is so rich in kindness and grace that he purchased our freedom with the blood of his Son and forgave our sins. Ephesians 1:7

[ ] **New life**

But because of his great love for us, God, who is rich in mercy, made us alive with Christ even when we were dead in transgressions—it is by grace you have been saved Ephesians 2:4-5

His divine power has given us everything we need for a godly life through our knowledge of Him who called us by His own glory and goodness. 2 Peter 1:3

[ ] **Eternal life**

For God so loved the world that he gave his only begotten son, that whoever believes in him will not perish but have eternal life. John 3:16

And, if that were the extent of it….that would be more than enough. Hallelujah.

But that's not all. Sadly, many of us fail to recognize (and walk in) the fact that we have changed "locations"…

Many, myself included, grew up believing and confessing that we were just "sinners saved by grace", and as such, we were to trudge through life carrying a heavy burden of sinfulness with the hope that someday we would be free when we went to be with Jesus in the sweet by and by. Inherent in that attitude was the assumption that we were unworthy servants who approach God with our tails appropriately tucked between our legs, with a reverent attitude of subjection, expecting crumbs from His table.

Also inherent in this attitude was the implication that God was "up there", or somewhere far from us, arms folded, waiting for us to clean up our act, live a life good enough, learn enough or do enough good things to convince Him to come "be with us" and come to our rescue. If we acted and prayed appropriately, God would be pleased with us and would answer our prayers…maybe. More subtly disguised was the greater falsehood that God's love and approval of us was somehow conditioned upon our behavior or performance.

Nothing could be further from the truth. Here is what God says about you…

1 John 3:1 - *See what great love the Father has lavished on us, that we should be called* **children of God**! *And that is what we are!*

28

Romans 8:15 - *The Spirit you received does not make you slaves, so that you live in fear again; rather, the Spirit you received brought about your* **adoption to sonship**. *And by him we cry, "Abba, Father."*

Romans 8:17 - *Now if we are children, then we are* **heirs—heirs** *of God and co-* **heirs** *with Christ*

Don't miss this…we are not orphans, hoping for a handout from a busy, reluctant, emotionally detached father…we are not slaves, with our heads down, undeserving of the attention and affection of our master. We are beloved children of a Father who loves us lavishly, completely and without any conditions. Sinners, yes, but totally redeemed by Jesus' blood, and now our Father only sees Jesus when He looks at us.

We are His kids. We are sons and daughters. Not stepsons and step-daughters. Not half sons/daughters…we are 100% sons/daughters. We are his heirs. All that He has is ours; not scraps from the table, but all-you-can-eat banquet food. Nothing is too good for His kids.

And I love this part…we have a Father who allows us to call him "dad" (*Abba*). This is the dad many of us have never had. A dad who welcomes us with open arms, kisses, the finest robe and the family crest ring…even when we stray away from him on occasion. (see Luke 15) This dad has forgiven all of our past misdeeds and has forgotten our independent, fist-in-your-face attitudes. His love is not contingent on us "cleaning up our act" or living a life that is somehow "good enough". He just loves us. Just as we are—mistakes and all.

This single truth, finally embraced many years after I first became a believer, has done more to draw me close to Him and compel me to walk daily with him than any other truth I can recall. Think on this for a minute or two:

> *"There is nothing you can do to make God love you any more; and there is nothing you can do to make Him love you less".*

He loves you. He likes you. He wants to be involved in every aspect of your life, because He loves you. The only reason you love Him at all, is because He first loved you. (1 John 4:19). You don't have to tap dance for God any longer. His love for you is not based on your behavior or performance. Don't let the enemy steal this from you.

Because of His love for us, we have also been given other amazing things:

A new position

> *And God raised us up with Christ and seated us with him in the heavenly realms in Christ Jesus.* Ephesians 2:6

> *Before long, the world will not see me anymore, but you will see me. Because I live, you also will live. On that day you will realize that I am in my Father, and you are in me, and I am in you.* John 14:19-20

Why does this matter?

It matters because of the preceding verses from Ephesians, Chapter 1: *and he (God) raised him (Christ) from the dead and seated him at his right hand in the heavenly places, far above all rule and authority and power and dominion, and above every name that is named, not only in this age but also in the one to come.* (Ephesians 1: 20-21)

Because we are "in Christ", and Christ is seated "*far above all rule and authority and power and dominion, and above every name that is named*", Paul goes on to tell us that: "*God raised us up with Christ and seated us with him in the heavenly realms in Christ* Jesus" (Ephesians 2:6).

Yes, we are physically walking this planet every day, but in the heavenly realm (remember Balaam and Elisha from Chapter Two), we (you and I) are seated (positioned) in Christ also "far above" the unseen rulers, authorities, powers and dominions that Satan uses to "kill, steal and destroy" (John 10:10) us and everything and everyone we care about.

So, it is crucial to remember "where" you sit....

Because of our position in Christ as His beloved children and heirs, we have also been given:

New power

> Ephesians 1:18-20 - *I pray that the eyes of your heart may be enlightened in order that you may know the hope to which he has called you, the riches of his glorious inheritance in his holy people, and his incomparably great power for us who believe. That power is the same as the mighty strength he exerted when he raised Christ from the dead and seated him at his right hand in the heavenly realms.*

> 1 John 4:4 - *You, dear children, are from God and have overcome them, because the one who is in you is greater than the one who is in the world.*

> 1 Corinthians 2:4 - *My message and my preaching were not with wise and persuasive words, but with a demonstration of the Spirit's power.*

> 2 Timothy 1:7 - *For the Spirit God gave us does not make us timid, but gives us power, love and self-discipline.*

Because Jesus has been raised by God's power and has been given a position of power above every other power and authority, and because we are "in Him" and He is in us - we have, in Christ, a new power over the forces of darkness that assail us.

But this is not simply a power to ask Jesus to invoke on our behalf. He gave His power to his disciples, the the seventy-two and to all of us who are his children. He equips us with power so that we can wield it in battle and push back those gates of hell he mentioned.

Jesus not only has all power, but He has all authority. He has not only allowed us to share his power, but has given us the authority to walk in that power.

New authority

Matthew 28:18 - *Then Jesus came to them and said, "All authority in heaven and on earth has been given to me.*

Luke 4:36 - *All the people were amazed and said to each other, "What words these are! With authority and power he gives orders to impure spirits and they come out!"*

Colossians 2:10 - *He is the head over every power and authority.*

Luke 9:1-2 *When Jesus had called the twelve together, he gave them power and authority to drive out all demons and to cure diseases, and he sent them out to proclaim the kingdom of God and to heal the sick.*

Luke 10:17-20 - *The seventy-two returned with joy and said, "Lord, even the demons submit to us in your name." He replied, "I saw Satan fall like lightning from heaven. I have given you authority to trample on snakes and scorpions and to overcome all the power of the enemy; nothing will harm you. However, do not rejoice that the spirits submit to you, but rejoice that your names are written in heaven."*

I draw your attention to one key phrase that we must also comprehend…."in your name" mentioned above. It is Jesus name, not ours, that makes demons tremble and leave. It is Jesus' name that is the name above all names. At Jesus' name every knee will bow in heaven and earth and under the earth. We must become fluent in invoking the powerful and matchless name of Jesus when wrestling with our enemies. We have every right and authority to use His name as His children and fellow heirs.

What has been missed by most believers, including myself, is the power associated with the name given to Jesus by God the Father. That name, **Jesus**, carries more power and authority than any other name and any other word in our vocabulary. Not Christ, not Savior, not even Lord…. Jesus. To speak his name is to wield the most powerful weapon in the universe.

Sadly, the name above all names has been mostly relegated to a "yours truly" or "sincerely yours" sign-off to our prayers. We have been duped. Yes, we are encouraged to pray "in Jesus' name" but I feel we have been deceived by not praying it more often and with the authority and power that it commands.

So, as followers of Jesus we have been given salvation, forgiveness and eternal life. We have also been given sonship, position, power and authority as his children. Much as in an earthly kingdom, the princes and princesses share the authority and power of the king because of their position as his children. Wherever they go, they represent the king and his rule. In the spiritual world, wherever we go, we bring and represent our Father, the King. We bring His kingdom and it's power and authority into every situation we face.

It is one thing to benefit from a position of authority and power. It is quite another to wield that authority and power when the enemy rises up against you. A police officer has authority because it has been granted to him by the city, state or national government. With that authority, he has the power to wave his arms and make traffic start, stop and obey his command. He speaks with authority when commanding people to stop or move along. But if those people choose not to obey that authority, and to defy, resist or assault that authority - the officer has weapons with which to enforce said authority.

New weapons

2 Corinthians 10:3-4 - *For though we live in the world, we do not wage war as the world does. The weapons we fight with are not the*

weapons of the world. On the contrary, they have divine power to demolish strongholds.

Yes, we are sinners saved by grace. Yes, God is holy and sovereign and deserves all our respect and reverence. But let's not also forget the truth that we are "new creations" in Christ, forgiven totally and loved unconditionally by a lavish Father who provides us with the authority, power and weapons we need to defeat the assaults of our mortal enemy and enjoy the abundant life He promised in Christ, both now and for eternity.

A chapter on these weapons is coming up soon…

So, why do we need a new position, complete with new power, authority and weapons?

Because our Father knew we were going to need them…all of them. Because war has been declared against us, and our enemy is formidable. What would you think of a father who allowed his children to live in a place, filled with evil, and not give them the ability to withstand and defeat it?

If we fail to recognize who we really are, and Whose we are - we will fail miserably when confronted by the enemy of our souls. Our position is "far above" him; our authority has been granted to us from the King of Kings Himself; our power is the same as that "which raised Christ from the dead"; and our weapons are "divinely powerful for the pulling down of strongholds": and we have been given permission and authority to invoke the most powerful name in the universe against every demonic force of darkness.

It doesn't get much better than that. As the church, we have got to not only pray "for" things - but also "against" things, if we are to see the power of God in our prayers, and God glorified.

But–the choice to engage our enemy, and utilize the authority, power and weapons we have been given…is ours to make.

"Christ in you, the hope of glory."
I'm not afraid of the devil. The devil can handle me - he's got judo I never
heard of.
But he can't handle the One to whom I am joined;
he can't handle the One to who I am united;
he can't handle the One whose nature dwells in my nature."
John Piper

CHAPTER FIVE

Feed the Dog

What are you thinking about?

⁓

Now that you know who you are, and what you have been given - it's time to dive deeper into the enemy's tactics and schemes. The more you know about them, the more easily you can recognize them and defeat them. Love this verse - *But solid food is for the mature, who by constant use have trained themselves to distinguish good from evil.* Hebrews 5:14

Here are some of the many ways God's Word shows us how our enemy assaults us and schemes against us and those we care most about:

- adversary (a force pushing against us and anything that brings God glory) - 1 Peter 5:8

- steals the Word - Matthew 13:19

- blinds the mind - 2 Corinthians 4:4

- deceives - 2 Corinthians 11:3

- torments - Acts 5:16

- murders (kills, snuffs out life/vitality/joy) - John 8:44

- thief - of what God has promised us (joy, peace, freedom…) - John 10:10

- inflicts - Luke 13:11

- lies - John 8:44

- accuses (to produce guilt, shame and discouragement) - Revelation 12:10

- speaks - thoughts - Matthew 15:19

- twists God's Word - Genesis 3:3

- tempts - Luke 4:2

Remember, the goal of everything Satan and his minions do - is the "kill, steal and destroy" (John 10:10) God's children and therefore, His glory.

He can't stand not being God and receiving the glory reserved only for Him. Since he knows that he has been overthrown and disarmed, his entire existence is focused on destroying God's glory by destroying his children.

His schemes are laser-focused on bringing down God's beloved children...you and me...and, our families, our finances, our witness, our ministries, our influence, our health, our peace, our joy, and our legacy.

He knows how the story ends (see Revelation 20). He knows his time is short...so, he is relentlessly at work to take down as many of us as possible before that time comes.

The Primary Battlefield...you must get this...

As you can see from the list at the beginning of this chapter...the primary venue for our "hand-to-hand combat" is our mind. The Bible refers to it as our "heart", and compels us to "watch over it" and "guard it" with all diligence. I don't know about you, but I never really thought about having a strategy for guarding my heart (mind, thoughts).

Look what God says about this:

Proverbs 4:23 - *above all else, guard your heart*

Proverbs 23:7 - *As a man thinks in his heart, so is he*

Romans 8:5-6 - *Those who live according to the flesh have their minds set on what the flesh desires; but those who live in accordance with the Spirit have their minds set on what the Spirit desires. The mind governed by the flesh is death, but the mind governed by the Spirit is life and peace.*

Romans 12:2 - *be transformed by the renewing of your mind*

2 Corinthians 10:5 - *We destroy arguments and every lofty opinion raised against the knowledge of God, and take every thought captive to obey Christ.*

In 2005, the National Science Foundation published an article showing that the average person has between 12,000 and 60,000 thoughts per day. That sounds like plenty of thoughts to me…but do I ever really think about what I am thinking about? What kind of thoughts are these? Are they helpful or harmful; evil or good; uplifting or defeating; frivolous or significant? And…do I just allow any and every thought to flow through my brain like water through a screen door….and never think about (analyze, capture) them?

As my good friend Zak once mentioned at our small group meeting…. "I need to think about what I think about". So simple, but so true. We all need to take his advice.

May I propose that our thoughts initiate from, and are influenced by, four primary sources…

- God (more specifically the Spirit of God)

- Satan

- Ourselves (flesh, sin nature)

- World (influenced by Satan, ie: culture, media, "friends")

The Bible speaks to these:

> *"For all that is in the* **world**, *the lust of the* **flesh**, *and the lust of the eyes, and the pride of life, is not of the Father, but is of the* **world**" 1 John 2:16

> *As for you, you were dead in your transgressions and sins, in which you used to live when you followed the ways of this* **world** *and of the* **ruler** *of the kingdom of the air, the* **spirit** *who is now at work in those who are disobedient. All of us also lived among them at one time, gratifying the cravings of our* **flesh** *and following its desires and thoughts. Like the rest, we were by nature deserving of wrath.* Ephesians 2:1-3

> *For those who are according to the* **flesh** *set their minds on the things of the* **flesh**, *but those who are according to the* **Spirit**, *the things of the* **Spirit**. *For the mind set on the* **flesh** *is death, but the mind set on the* **Spirit** *is life and peace, because the mind set on the* **flesh** *is hostile toward God; for it does not subject itself to the law of God, for it is not even able to do so, and those who are in the* **flesh** *cannot please God.* Romans 8:5-8

> *I will bless the Lord who has counseled me; Indeed, my* **mind** *instructs me in the night.* Psalm 16:7

> *And He said to him, "'You shall love the Lord your God with all your heart, and with all your soul, and with all your* **mind**.' Matthew 22:37

> *And do not be conformed to this world, but be transformed by the renewing of your* **mind**, *so that you may prove what the will of God is, that which is good and acceptable and perfect.* Romans 12:2

> *…in whose case the god of this world has blinded the* **minds** *of the unbelieving so that they might not see the light of the gospel of the glory of Christ, who is the image of God.* 2 Corinthians 4:4

But I am afraid that, as the serpent deceived Eve by his craftiness, your **minds** *will be led astray from the simplicity and purity of devotion to Christ.* 2 Corinthians 11:3

Set your **mind** *on the things above, not on the things that are on earth.* Colossians 3:2

*These are the ones who cause divisions, worldly-***minded***, devoid of the Spirit.* Jude 1:19

There are over 160 Bible references to "mind", and these are but a few. Needless to say, what is going on in our mind is of great concern to God and should be to us.

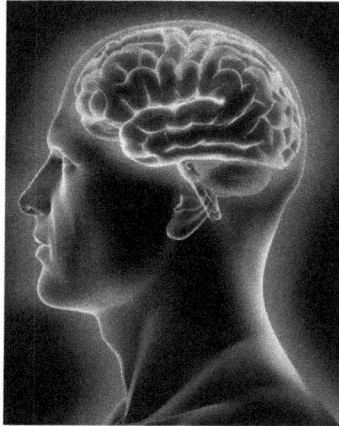

Before we were saved, God says:

the god of this world had blinded our mind so that we could not see the light of the gospel. 2 Corinthians 4:4

we were dead in our transgressions and sins, in which we used to live when we followed the ways of this world and of the ruler of the kingdom of the air, the spirit who is now at work in those who are disobedient. All of us also lived among them at one time, gratifying the cravings of our flesh and following its desires and thoughts. Like the rest, we were by nature deserving of wrath. Ephesians 2:1-3

Our minds were blinded and we were spiritually dead to God. Our thoughts were focused on gratifying ourselves, enjoying our independence and following the ways and "wisdom" of the world around us. Little did we know, there was an evil, sinister force behind it all, influencing our thoughts and actions.

Then, solely by His grace, God provided a way out of the darkness and into His light. Accepting His offer of forgiveness, sonship and eternal life, through Christ's sacrificial death on the cross and subsequent resurrection, means we not only can enjoy an eternity in heaven, but we can have victory over Satan's destructive thoughts and schemes.

We now have the Spirit of God living inside of us, and His desire is to lead us away from our old, sin-filled life (thoughts, actions, influences, dangers) toward a new life, filled with peace, joy, power and freedom.

And that's when the war begins.

You see, even though God's Spirit now resides in us and is always available in our mind/heart to lead us closer to God and away from the enemy, our own spirit, full of years of sinful thoughts, actions and influence didn't go away. We now have two spirits at work in our mind.

There is a story of a man from the city whose car broke down on a country road while traveling. He walked to a nearby farm and saw an elderly farmer casually watching two dogs fighting - one white, one black. Startled by the unusual sight, the man asked the farmer, "which one usually wins"?

The gruff old farmer replied, "whichever one I feed".

A simple story to illustrate a powerful truth. Do any of these sound familiar?

And I know that nothing good lives in me, that is, in my sinful nature. I want to do what is right, but I can't. Romans 7:18

But there is another power within me that is at war with my mind. This power makes me a slave to the sin that is still within me. Romans 7:23

For the sinful nature is always hostile to God. It never did obey God's laws, and it never will. Romans 8:7

The battle for our minds, which in turn will control our actions and lives, will be won by which influence we decide to "feed". Will we, by our choices, feed the thoughts and influences hurled at us by the world, our flesh and the enemy himself? Or, will we choose to pursue and "feed" the thoughts and influences available to us by our Father God, Who …

– *makes all things work together for good, for all those who love Him and those who are called according to his purpose.* Romans 8:28

– *has granted to us all things that pertain to life and godliness.* 2 Peter 1:3

– *will supply every need of yours according to his riches in glory in Christ.* Phil.4:19

– allow us to bear *the fruit of the Spirit - love, joy, peace, patience, kindness, goodness, faithfulness, gentleness and self-control.* Galatians 5:22

Paul sums it up well in Romans 8:6 - *So letting your sinful nature control your mind leads to death. But letting the Spirit control your mind leads to life and peace.*

All of us want *life and peace.* The hard part is consistently feeding our mind with God's Word, proactively thinking about what we think about throughout the day, and then, choosing to *take any thoughts captive* that aren't from God… and that takes work.

If you haven't developed a strategy for guarding your heart (mind)…now is the time.

As someone thinks within himself, so is he. Proverbs 23:7

CHAPTER SIX

The Battlefield - continued

Taking captives

∽

The weapons of our warfare are not carnal but mighty in God for pulling down strongholds, casting down arguments and every high thing that exalts itself against the knowledge of God, bringing every thought into captivity to the obedience of Christ.

2 Corinthians 10:4-5

Take a walk with me and let's look under the hood of this crucial passage:

1. We have been given weapons. Why? Because we are at war and they are expected to be used in our warfare. Without weapons we are….defenseless in warfare. We have been given weapons (by God) for our own protection and to achieve victory.

2. Our weapons are not "carnal". They are not man-made, or of our own making. If they were, they would hold no power against a diabolical, spiritual enemy.

3. Our weapons are "mighty". They are "supremely powerful", effective and capable.

4. Our weapons are mighty "in God" or "through God"...not in ourselves or through our own efforts or strength. God provides the weapons and endows them with His divine power and effectiveness.

5. Our weapons are designed to "pull down strongholds", "cast down arguments (imaginations)", and cast down "every high thing that exalts itself against the knowledge of God".

6. *Pulling down* equals "demolish". God's weapons are designed to utterly demolish Satan's strongholds (fortresses) that may exist in our lives. We will discuss how these get erected.

   Cast down equals "demolish with violence". Our weapons are capable of smashing into little pieces the following:

   Every high/lofty thing that exalts itself against the knowledge (knowing) of God. Every thought, idea, imagining, excuse or reason that may enter our mind with the intent of leading us away from knowing God, His will, direction, intent, love and plan.

Thoughts enter our mind all day long. We cannot stop them from coming. What we can train ourselves to do, however, is to be more sensitive to what they are and where they are from. Here are a few common examples:

- I feel good this morning. This is going to be a great day.

- I didn't sleep so well. This is probably going to be an awful day.

- Why is she whining all the time? I can't wait for her to grow up.

- This dress is way too tight. I need to lose some weight. I look like a slob.

- What a moron? Doesn't he know how to drive?

- Why does he always talk this way to me? I deserve better than this.

- I can't seem to win at anything. I am such a failure.

The list goes on, and on...and on. All day...every day.

We can't stop them, but what if we could "file" them away in their proper place. Is this thought a positive one, or negative? Uplifting or depressing? Encouraging or discouraging? Hopeful of fearful? Does it bring me peace, or anxiety? Does it draw me closer to the Lord, or to my spouse/family–or intend to drive me away?

You get the idea.

The world (under the influence and control of Satan) sends thoughts of fear, anxiety, hopelessness, negativity, division, sensuality, etc.

The flesh sends thoughts of selfishness, self gratification, and thoughts around "what about me - what do I want - what do I deserve - what do I need–what is my agenda" - etc.

God, by His Spirit, sends thoughts of love, peace, joy, patience, kindness, goodness, others-centered, hope, positivity, holiness, unity, and what brings God glory.

If we take the time to think about what we are thinking about, we can better discern the source of a thought, and take it captive. Will we receive it, agree with it and act on it...or cast it down as from the enemy of our soul?

Let me illustrate this concept...

CHAPTER SEVEN

Eve vs. Jesus

A Tale of Two Temptations

〜

A GREAT LESSON ON GUARDING your heart (mind) and taking your thoughts captive is found by looking at how Eve handled her encounter with Satan and how Jesus handled his.

Eve knew God's word - at least what God said to Adam, her husband. Adam had been told directly by God …

> *And the Lord God commanded him, "You may eat freely from every tree of the garden, but you must not eat from the tree of the knowledge of good and evil; for in the day that you eat of it, you will surely die." Genesis 2:16*

Adam, no doubt, had relayed that message to Eve, because she repeated it to Satan during their encounter. Here is the record of that encounter from Genesis 3:1-6:

> *Now the serpent was more crafty than any beast of the field that the Lord God had made. And he said to the woman, "Did God really say, 'You must not eat from any tree in the garden?'"*
> *The woman answered the serpent, "We may eat the fruit of the trees of the garden, but about the fruit of the tree in the middle*

of the garden, God has said, 'You must not eat of it or touch it, or you will die.'"

"You will not surely die," the serpent told her. "For God knows that in the day you eat of it, your eyes will be opened and you will be like God, knowing good and evil."

When the woman saw that the tree was good for food and pleasing to the eyes, and that it was desirable for obtaining wisdom, she took the fruit and ate it.

Poor Eve. She was way out matched by the most beautiful, yet diabolical creature ever created. No one would blame her for engaging such a stunning creature, but she had no clue what she was up against. Satan was a pro at deception, twisting God's words and the *"father of lies"* (John 8:44). She was a newbie (literally), innocent and naive…so, she engaged him in what she thought was a harmless conversation.

Satan, as is typical, leads with *"did God really say…"* to make her begin to question what she heard and what God really meant. Now, she is pondering not only what she heard from Adam, but also the words from the serpent's mouth. She responds with the only knowledge she has on the matter. Satan again casts doubt on God's intent and His heart.

Then it happened. Somewhere between Genesis 3, verse 5 and verse 6…. Eve took time to ponder what Satan had said, accept it as true and then make an agreement with it. Once she agreed, it was time to take action - so, she "saw" the fruit in an entirely different light. Notice, it is now ""good", "pleasing" and "desirable", where just a short time earlier it was just a piece of forbidden fruit. She was hooked. She took it and willingly ate a bite and gave it to her passive, present husband and he ate too.

The results were catastrophic…

In contrast, let's look in Matthew, Chapter 4, at a similar scene where Jesus is being tempted by the same tempter…

*Then Jesus was led by the Spirit into the wilderness to be tempted by
the devil. After fasting forty days and forty nights, He was hungry.
The tempter came to Him and said, "If you are the Son of God, tell
these stones to become bread."*

After 40 days of fasting, Jesus was no doubt hungry…starving…and
vulnerable, and the enemy knows where and when we are most vulnerable.
So, he challenges Jesus' deity and also tempts him to satisfy his natural
appetite by using the power of that deity. It all sounds so logical…I'm God,
I'm hungry…make bread…end of hunger.

It is at this point that the comparison with Eve takes a hard right turn…

Eve pondered. She engaged. She would have thought that making bread
out of stones when you're hungry made perfect sense.

Jesus didn't ponder, he didn't engage. He recognized the temptation for
what it was and spoke truth against the enemy's deceptive scheme.

*But Jesus answered, "It is written: 'Man shall not live on bread alone,
but on every word that comes from the mouth of God.'"*

Two more times the devil tempts, and two more times Jesus models
for us the most effective rebuttal… "*It is written…*"

In verse eleven we are told the conclusion of the battle…*Then the devil
left Him, and angels came and ministered to Him.*

So…what is the lesson here?

We will all be tempted, regularly, daily - by the same diabolical enemy
who tempted Eve and Jesus (and everyone else). He is not kidding. His lies,
deceptions and schemes are all meant to "kill, steal and destroy" us and
everything and everybody we love. He is out to "devour".

Eve - listened to his voice and his reasoning long enough for them to
make sense to her. Once she agreed with the lies, she acted on them - she
turned her back on God's love and His truth and deliberately ate.

Jesus - heard the enemy's voice, but refused to engage or believe his lies.
He did not stop to ponder and agreed only with what God's Word (truth)

says. He immediately spoke the truth in response to the temptation, and kept it up until the enemy left him.

So, what about you? What about me? What do we do when tempted?

Do we listen, engage, ponder and tend to agree - or, do we know enough of God's truth to immediately refute and reject the "opportunity" at hand?

Here's what that looks like:

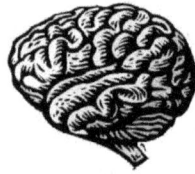

Hear

Receive
Accept/Reject

Process
Ponder/Entertain

Agreement

Action
Act/Speak

I believe this is what Paul meant when he wrote,

We demolish arguments and every pretension that sets itself up against the knowledge of God, and we take captive every thought to make it obedient to Christ. 2 Corinthians 10:5

As mature believers, we need to learn to *demolish* Satan's *arguments* and *take our thoughts captive.* We need to think more about what we think about and discern where thoughts are coming from and what to do with them. If the enemy can get us to ponder and eventually agree with his lies, we will end up like Eve…defeated.

We also need to fill our minds with God's Word so, like Jesus, we can quickly respond to the tempter–"it is written". He cannot speak anything but lies, so we must equip ourselves to recognize them (compare them with the truth) and then speak truth into the situation.

The word of God is *alive and powerful…* - Hebrews 4:12

The word of God is *the sword of the Spirit* - Ephesians 6:17

One of our primary weapons against the schemes of the enemy is the Word. We must, however, know it and be willing to wield it in battle.

———

One of our sons attended high school with a beautiful young girl who experienced this firsthand. Although she was attractive and thin, she went through a very hard and painful season in high school where she would look in a mirror and hear the words (thoughts)–"you're fat", "you're ugly", etc. She made the mistake of listening to those thoughts and eventually agreeing with and acting on them.

She began a long battle with anorexia, which nearly ended her life. She became emaciated and frail, yet all the while having the same thoughts when she looked in her mirror. She would have become another Christian young woman who the enemy devoured had she not sought and received powerful Christian counsel. She is alive today because she learned to take her thoughts captive and wield the powerful sword of the Word.

———

My wife and I had a close, longtime friend whose outcome was much different and devastating. A successful businessman, he was a strong Christian, a strong Bible teacher and pillar in his local church. A loving husband and father, he was greatly admired by all of us.

After a series of physical and business setbacks, the enemy seized upon the opportunity at the precise moment of weakness and desperation. The voices (thoughts) in his head were no doubt strong…"you're a failure", "you'll never recover from this", "your family would be better off if you were dead"…sadly, he pondered those thoughts and finally agreed with the lies…and he spiraled downward.

Despite counsel from close friends, family and pastors–they found him unresponsive in his office.

Tragedy in our own circle…to friends of ours…to a beloved Christian family.

Why? How does this happen?

None of us is immune. Remember - war has been declared and we have an enemy who never sleeps, never rests, never takes a vacation. His goal 24/7/365 is to *"kill, steal and destroy"* us…to *"devour"* us…to *"steal"* our life, our health, our mental health, our joy, our finances, our marriage, our kids, our witness and our heritage.

———

So, how do we recognize these assaults and deal with them before it's too late?

The Bible, once again, is very clear…

Be alert, be on watch! Your enemy, the devil, roams around like a roaring lion, looking for someone to devour. 1 Peter 5:8

But there is another power within me that is at war with my mind. Romans 7:23

And do not be conformed to this world, but be transformed by the renewing of your mind. Romans 12:2

Above all else, guard your heart (mind), for everything you do flows from it. Proverbs 4:23

Recognize there is an all-out assault being waged on our mind. The intent of this assault is to devour/destroy us. We must stay alert and watchful (think about what we think about), and get serious about renewing our minds daily with God's Word... and be deliberate about guarding our heart.

Here is another way to recognize an assault that may be helpful...

The fruit (evidence) of walking in the Spirit is love, joy, peace, patience, kindness, goodness, faithfulness, gentleness and self-control - Galatians 5:22-23

If we are doing the basics as believers by walking in the Spirit...by reading His Word diligently, by fasting and praying, and listening to His voice and following Him–there will be fruit naturally occurring in our lives as a result.

Jesus reminded us of this naturally-occurring principle in John 15:4...*Remain in me, as I also remain in you. No branch can bear fruit by itself; it must remain in the vine. Neither can you bear fruit unless you remain in me.*

As Christ-followers, we are exhorted to "abide" or "remain" in Christ. If we choose to do so, we will experience the natural fruit (result) of that abiding...namely love, joy, peace, etc.

So what if, instead of love–you are feeling bitterness, selfishness or unforgiveness?

What about sorrow, hopelessness or despair instead of joy?

What if our thoughts are filled with tension, strife and busyness instead of peace?

Impatience, quick temper and anxiety instead of patience?

Unkindness, sarcasm or mean-spiritedness in the place of kind-ness…you get the idea.

When we find these contrary thoughts harassing us instead of the Lord's promised "peace", "rest" and the other fruit…..then you are being attacked. You need to immediately recognize it for what it is, and remember you are *not wrestling/struggling against flesh and blood, but against the rulers, against the authorities, against the powers of this dark world and against the spiritual forces of evil in the heavenly realms.* Ephesians 6:12.

That is the moment when we must also realize we are most likely not walking "in the Spirit"–trusting, resting, listening/obeying, etc.–and get reconnected to the "vine". We must know and speak the truth of God's Word to our attacker, and demand he leave. Another promise and truth to stand on is this–

> *Submit yourselves, then, to God. Resist the devil, and he will flee from you.* James 4:7

(Remember from Chapter 2 - resist him out loud, as he cannot read your mind or hear your thoughts…and he "will" (not "might") flee. So, walk in step with the Spirit (submit), speak God's truth when attacked (resist)..and watch as the enemy flees.

Hopefully, these ideas will help you better recognize and resist the assaults coming against your thought life. Ask God to make you more aware of your thought life and to teach you how to better recognize and resist the enemy.

When we do realize an attack, we need to be able to draw from our arsenal of weapons, and stop it in it's tracks…like Jesus did.

Let's take a deeper dive into what other weapons we have in our arse-nal…

"We are not walking in the Word
if our thoughts are opposite of what it says.
We are not walking in the Word
if we are not thinking in the Word."
– Joyce Meyer

CHAPTER EIGHT

The Arsenal

Fighting From Victory

﹏

Today, we do not fight for victory, we fight from victory.
– Watchman Nee

Looking at Jesus' approach is a great place to start as we investigate the *weapons of our warfare* as Paul reminds us in 2 Corinthians 10:4.

Reminder–we need weapons because we are at war. This war began before man was ever created but is still raging all around us. Jesus knew it, and came to win the war by His death and resurrection. He disarmed the enemy and took back the rulership and authority once given to Adam and Eve. He didn't, however, destroy Satan's presence or influence on earth. While that will happen one day, we must learn to rule and reign as His children while we remain on this planet - and not allow our enemy to take back any ground in our lives.

- War has been declared - Revelation 12:17

- Jesus came to destroy the work of Satan - 1 John 3:8

- He disarmed our enemy - Colossians 2:15

- Jesus took back His authority /rulership position - Ephesians 1:19-23 / Matthew 28:18

· He gave us back the authority and rulership we once had - Luke 10:17-20

Satan knows he has been defeated and disarmed. He also knows what is written about his eventual eternal demise. His time on earth is short, so he and his forces are working overtime to "kill, steal and destroy" as many lives as possible in the time they have left. War has been declared on all Christians. Thank goodness we have everything we need to live victoriously in the middle of that war.

Let's take a closer look at what we have been given as His children and heirs…

Weapons

The weapons of our warfare are not the weapons of the world. Instead, they have divine power to demolish strongholds. 2 Corinthians 10:4

Don't miss that–we need (and have been given) weapons, and these weapons have divine power…for a purpose…to demolish.

Our primary weapons:

The Word of God

As we have discussed previously, Jesus' response to Satan when tempted was an immediate "it is written". Jesus spoke, he spoke the truth and power of God's Word, and he didn't ask God to take the temptation away. Jesus knew that God had given him the Word and that it was powerful (Hebrews 4:12). He spoke that Word because he also knew the enemy could not hear his thoughts. He didn't ask his Father to do it for him because he knew he had been given the ability and authority to be victorious in this type of confrontation.

Takeaway–we too have been given the powerful Word of God with which to resist the devil. We are told that if we resist him, he "will" flee. We know to speak the Word aloud in order for it to be effective. It should be obvious that if we don't know the Word, we can't speak it. Knowing what to say is critical. (more to come on that)....

Satan's number-one objective is to destroy our joy of faith. We have an offensive weapon in the sword of the Spirit, the Word of God (Eph. 6:17). But what many Christians fail to realize is that we can't draw the sword from someone else's scabbard. If we don't wear it, we can't wield it. If the Word of God does not abide in us (Jn. 15:7), we will reach for it in vain when the enemy strikes. But if we do wear it, if it lives within us, what mighty warriors we can be!
John Piper

Practical - Let's say you, or someone in your household is wrestling with fear. What does the Word say?

God is our refuge and strength, a very present help in trouble. Therefore, we will not fear... - Psalm 46:1-2

for God did not give us a spirit of fear, but of power, and of love, and of a sound mind - 2 Timothy 1:7

There is no fear in love. But perfect love drives out fear - 1 John 4:18

So, if there is no fear in love because God is love....and fear is not from God....and He is our refuge and strength when we start to become fearful.... we must conclude that fear must come from somewhere else - you guessed it...from our enemy.

Knowing the truth from God's Word, we can now take these fearful thoughts captive and speak the truth into the situation and into our hearts. We can declare our resistance to the enemy's attempt to torment us with fear, and he must flee.

Like Jesus, we don't ask God to make us less fearful, we take out our sword and vanquish the enemy's scheme. It is our right as His children, and as such, we have the authority to do so.

More truth to know regarding the Word of God–

Then you will know the truth, and the truth will set you free. - John 8:32

So faith comes from hearing, and hearing by the word of God. - Romans 10:17

For the word of the cross is foolishness to those who are perishing, but to us who are being saved it is the power of God. - 1 Corinthians 1:18

For the word of God is living and active and sharper than any two-edged sword, and piercing as far as the division of soul and spirit, of both joints and marrow, and able to judge the thoughts and intentions of the heart. - Hebrews 4:12

"I have written to you, young men, because you are strong, and the Word of God abides in you, and you have overcome the wicked one.". - 1 John 2:14

The Authority of God

One of the most amazing things about Jesus' death, resurrection and ascension is that by doing so, he paid the just penalty for the sin of Adam and Eve (as well as our own) and took back the rule and authority that they abdicated to Satan at their fall.

I ask that the eyes of your heart may be enlightened, so that you may know the hope of His calling, the riches of His glorious inheritance in the saints, and the surpassing greatness of His power to us who believe. These are in accordance with the working of His mighty strength, which He exerted in Christ when He raised Him from the dead and seated Him at His right hand in the heavenly realms, far above all rule and authority, power and dominion, and every name that is named, not only in this age, but also in the one to come. And God put everything under His feet and made Him head over everything for the church, which is His body, the fullness of Him who fills all in all. Ephesians 1:18-23

Even though Christ humbled himself to become a man, he still retained the authority he had as God's son, and heir. He exercised that authority when addressing evil spirits (see Luke 4:36), when healing people with physical needs, when raising Lazarus from the dead, and when calming a storm on the Sea of Galilee. As Creator, he retained authority over his creation.

All authority in heaven and earth has been given to me. - Matthew 28:18

What is most humbling is that he also had all authority to stop his excruciating torture and execution as well....but chose not to because of his love for us.... Wow.

Remember this interaction when Satan was tempting Jesus in the wilderness ?(Luke 4:5-7)

Then the devil led Him up to a high place and showed Him in an instant all the kingdoms of the world. "I will give You authority over all these kingdoms and all their glory," he said. "For it has been relinquished to me, and I can give it to anyone I wish. So if You worship me, it will all be Yours."

Adam and Eve had *relinquished* the authority they had been given by God over all the kingdoms of the earth when they chose to turn their backs on God and seek their own way. Satan now had authority over these earthly kingdoms, and they were his to give away if he chose.

So while Jesus retained ultimate authority over all created things, he allowed Satan and his minions to exercise authority to reign over the earth.

At his death, Jesus proclaimed, "It is finished" announcing the end of his mission on earth to pay the price for our sin, paving the way for us to receive eternal life - and also to take back the spiritual authority on earth, *relinquished* to Satan in the Garden.

> *The reason the Son of God appeared was to destroy the works of the devil.* 1 John 3:8b

You see, Jesus had a plan for that authority...and it involves us.

The "Great Commission" given by Jesus to his disciples is very familiar to most believers...

> *"All authority in heaven and on earth has been given to Me. Therefore go and make disciples of all nations, baptizing them in the name of the Father, and of the Son, and of the Holy Spirit, and teaching them to obey all that I have commanded you. And surely I am with you always, even to the end of the age."* - Matthew 28:18-20

While we would all do well to heed Jesus' commission to "go" and "make disciples" of all nations, we should also take note of his earlier commissioning of his disciples and even a larger group of followers, called the "seventy-two"...

> *And calling His twelve disciples to Him, Jesus gave them authority over unclean spirits, so that they could drive them out and heal every disease and sickness.*
>
> *These twelve Jesus sent out with the following instructions: "Do not go onto the road of the Gentiles or enter any town of the Samaritans. Go rather to the lost sheep of Israel. As you go, preach this message: 'The kingdom of heaven is near.' Heal the sick, raise the dead, cleanse the lepers, drive out demons. Freely you have received; freely give."* - Matthew 10:1, 5-8

Then Jesus called the twelve together and gave them power and authority over all demons, and power to cure diseases. And He sent them out to proclaim the kingdom of God and to heal the sick.
Luke 9:1-2

After this, the Lord appointed seventy-two others and sent them two by two ahead of Him to every town and place He was about to visit. And He told them, "The harvest is plentiful, but the workers are few. Ask the Lord of the harvest, therefore, to send out workers into His harvest.

The seventy-two returned with joy and said, "Lord, even the demons submit to us in Your name." So He told them, "I saw Satan fall like lightning from heaven. See, I have given you authority to tread on snakes and scorpions, and over all the power of the enemy. Nothing will harm you. Nevertheless, do not rejoice that the spirits submit to you, but rejoice that your names are written in heaven."
Luke 10:1-2, 17-20

From these texts, it seems clear that part of Jesus' plan to take back the earthly authority *relinquished* by Adam and Eve, was to pass it on to his disciples, his followers, his church.

In Matthew 16, Jesus told Peter that he would *build his church, and the gates of hell would not prevail against it.* Obviously, hell has no literal entrance with gates, and according to Strong's *Greek Concordance and Greek Lexicon of New Testament*, the Greek word πύλης (gates) in antiquity was also used to indicate *authority* and *power*.

As we have just read, part of Jesus' plan for coming to earth was to destroy the works of the devil (1 John 3:8), and to disciple the men who would begin an invasion against the influence, authority and power of hell...the church.

> *"Do not think that I have come to bring peace to the earth. I have not come to bring peace, but a sword.* Matthew 10:34

65

Friend, as children of God and joint heirs with Christ, we have been enlisted in the great war. We have been given armor (a uniform), divinely powerful weapons, authority over all the power of the enemy and a commission from our Lord. The cruise ship metaphor has sunk…it's time to learn how to take back enemy territory, and kick in a few gates….

For the kingdom of God is not a matter of talk, but of power.
1 Corinthians 4:20

The Armor of God (Ephesians 6:10-18) - *Finally, be strong in the Lord and in his mighty power. Put on the full armor of God, so that you can take your stand against the devil's schemes. For our struggle is not against flesh and blood, but against the rulers, against the authorities, against the powers of this dark world and against the spiritual forces of evil in the heavenly realms. Therefore put on the full armor of God, so that when the day of evil comes, you may be able to stand your ground, and after you have done everything, to stand. Stand firm then, with the belt of truth buckled around your waist, with the breastplate of righteousness in place, and with your feet fitted with the readiness that comes from the gospel of peace. In addition to all this, take up the shield of faith, with which you can extinguish all the flaming arrows of the evil one. Take the helmet of salvation and the sword of the Spirit, which is the word of God. And pray in the Spirit on all occasions with all kinds of prayers and requests.*

It is worth noting that Paul encourages us to *be strong*, not in our own might or power, but *in Jesus and in His power*. Since we have a choice in the matter, we are exhorted to *put on the armor*…and not only that, but to put on the *full* (entire) armor - which indicates we don't have to if we don't want to. We are also exhorted to *stand firm*, in what we have already been given - His truth, His righteousness and His commission.

Paul then encourages us to make the decision to *take up* the helmet of salvation (protecting our minds/thoughts) and *take* the sword of the Spirit, which is God's Word.

As already mentioned, knowing His truth, wielding it (verbally) in battle, and acting on what He tells us - are all crucial elements included in his definition of being *strong in the Lord*. Lastly, but not least, we are to *pray* in accordance with the Spirit on all occasions, which we are told later in 1 Thessalonians 5:17 …means *"without ceasing"*.

Personal: That verse is quite revealing to me. If prayer is indeed a dialogue and not a monologue, and God tells us to pray "without ceasing" - then He is also willing to communicate with us unceasingly. He's listening, His speaking, He's engaged - unceasingly available to you and me. I love that.

Clearly the armor of God embodies both defensive and offensive features. Armor, belts, breastplates and helmets protect vital organs. Shields stop painful, flaming arrows launched at us continually by our enemy. Our sword (God's Word) is *sharper than any two-edged sword* , and is our primary offensive weapon in battle, as we have discussed. While debate exists as to whether or not prayer is mentioned as part of this set of armor, it is no doubt included as another form of offensive weapon when spoken in agreement with the Spirit's plan and power.

The Blood of Jesus (Revelation 12:13) - *They overcame him (Satan) by the blood of the Lamb, by the word of their testimony, and they loved not their own lives unto death.*

Because of Jesus' shed blood and death on the cross, Satan's lies and accusations mean nothing to us and have absolutely no power or influence over us (unless we allow them). Jesus has already paid the penalty our sins deserved. We are made completely righteous by the substitutionary work of Jesus on the cross.

> *In fact, the law requires that nearly everything be cleansed with blood, and without the shedding of blood there is no forgiveness.* - Hebrews 9:22
>
> *The next day John saw Jesus coming toward him and said, "Look, the Lamb of God, who takes away the sin of the world!* - John 1:29

Jesus was the sacrificial Lamb who was slain for our sin. His blood washed away our guilt, justified us completely before God and offers us redemption and eternal life in the presence of God.

Satan is called *the accuser of the brethren* (Revelation 12:10) and he relentlessly accuses us of past sins and mistakes in an ongoing effort to wear us down, make us doubt our salvation and our worth, and render us impotent for the kingdom and glory of God.

Thanks to the blood of the Lamb, we can immediately and consistently refute Satan's accusations (lies) with the truth that we are *bought with a price* (1 Corinthians 6:20*), redeemed* by His blood (Galatians 3:13) and forever a beloved and *forgiven* member of God's family. (Galatians 4:6)

David wrote of Jesus' sacrificial death in Psalm 103:12 - *as far as the east is from the west, so far has he removed our transgressions from us.*

As the old hymn says so well–"What can wash away my sin; nothing but the blood of Jesus".

We would do well to remember often the blood Jesus voluntarily shed at the cross on our behalf. He took the punishment for our sin, and shed His blood so we can be seen as blameless before God.

The Power of Prayer

Until you know that life is war, you do not know what prayer is for. –John Piper

Prayer is a dialogue, not a monologue.

Prayer is a two-way conversation between God and His children.

Prayer is spiritual communication between man and God, a two-way relationship in which man should not only talk to God but also listen to Him.

God's Word not only encourages us to pray, but exhorts us to pray believing God will answer our prayer....

Is anyone among you sick? Let him call for the elders of the church, and let them pray over him, anointing him with oil in the name of the Lord. And the prayer of faith will save the one who is sick, and the Lord will raise him up. - James 5:14-16

Therefore I tell you, whatever you ask in prayer, believe that you have received it, and it will be yours. - Mark 11:24

Whatever you ask in my name, this I will do, that the Father may be glorified in the Son. If you ask me anything in my name, I will do it. - John 14:13-14

But he must ask in faith, without doubting, because he who doubts is like a wave of the sea, blown and tossed by the wind. That man should not expect to receive anything from the Lord. - James 1:6-7

God's Word also reminds us that prayer is incredibly powerful....

Elijah was a man with a nature like ours, and he prayed earnestly that it would not rain, and it did not rain on the earth for three years and six months. Then he prayed again, and the sky poured rain and the earth produced its fruit. - James 5:17-18

And it happened that the father of Publius was lying in bed afflicted with recurrent fever and dysentery; and Paul went in to see him and after he had prayed, he laid his hands on him and healed him. - Acts 28:8

When they came down to him, Elisha prayed to the Lord and said, "Strike this people with blindness, I pray." So He struck them with blindness according to the word of Elisha. - 2 Kings 6:18

"You don't have enough faith," Jesus told them. "I tell you the truth, if you had faith even as small as a mustard seed, you could say to this mountain, 'Move from here to there,' and it would move. Nothing would be impossible." - Matthew 17:20

Why are we reluctant to involve God at the very first sign of a fight? Is there something innately inside us that feels we can "do it myself"? If you're like me, you have a tendency to try several of your own ideas and options before the proverbial light goes on and you remember…."oh yeah….maybe I should pray about this". Remember John 15:5? *Without me* (Jesus), *you can do nothing.* SO, why do we hesitate going to Him immediately.

My wife and I bought a small plaque that greets us when we walk through the door to our home. It reads…PRAY FIRST.

A simple but powerful, ongoing reminder of what should be our first response and privilege as God's beloved.

So friends, we have all the weapons we need at our disposal. The "same power that raised Christ from the dead", the Spirit of God, literally lives inside us…and we have been given spiritual weapons that are "divinely powerful".

What else do we need?

There's one more thing you have to know…

CHAPTER NINE

Jesus

Name Above All Names

⁓

Therefore God exalted Him to the highest place and gave Him the name above all names, that at the name of Jesus every knee should bow, in heaven and on earth and under the earth, and every tongue confess that Jesus Christ is Lord to the glory of God the Father. - Philippians 2:9-11

Some of the most recognizable names in:

- **sports** = Mantle, Ruth, Koufax, Peyton, Simpson, Ronaldo, Messi, Jordan, Kobe, Woods, Nicklaus, Federer, Ali, etc.

- **business** = Disney, Walton, Buffet, Ford, Rockefeller, Zuckerberg, Bezos, Gates, Edison, Winfrey, Carnegie, Musk, etc.

- **politics** = Kennedy, Churchill, Lincoln, Gandhi, Reagan, Roosevelt, Thatcher, King, Bush, Putin, Washington, Clinton, etc.

But, no name that has ever been, or ever will be, can compare to the name given to the baby born in a manger in Bethlehem over 2000 years ago…Jesus. No other name in heaven or on earth makes demons tremble with fear and run for their lives…. Jesus.

The most powerful weapon ever given to the disciples, the seventy-two, and to all of us who come after them…is a name…Jesus.

———————

Later as they were eating, Jesus appeared to the eleven and rebuked them for their unbelief and hardness of heart, because they did not believe those who had seen Him after He had risen. And He said to them, "Go into all the world and preach the gospel to every creature. Whoever believes and is baptized will be saved, but whoever does not believe will be condemned.

And these signs will accompany those who believe: <u>In my name</u> they will drive out demons; they will speak in new tongues; they will pick up snakes with their hands, and if they drink any deadly poison, it will not harm them; they will lay their hands on the sick, and they will be made well." - Mark 16:14-18

The seventy-two returned with joy and said, "Lord, even the demons submit to us <u>in your name</u>." - Luke 10:17

One afternoon Peter and John were going up to the temple at the hour of prayer, the ninth hour. And a man who was lame from birth was being carried to the temple gate called Beautiful, where he was put every day to beg from those entering the temple courts. When he saw Peter and John about to enter the temple, he asked them for money. Peter looked directly at him, as did John. "Look at us!" said Peter. So the man gave them his attention, expecting to receive something from them. But Peter said, "Silver or gold I do not have, but what I have I give you: <u>In the name of Jesus Christ</u> of Nazareth, get up and walk!"

By faith in the name of Jesus, this man whom you see and know has been made strong. It is <u>Jesus' name</u> and the faith that comes through Him that has given him this complete healing in your presence. - Acts 3:1-6, 16

Then Peter, filled with the Holy Spirit, said to them: "Rulers and elders of the people! If we are being called to account today for an act of kindness shown to a man who was lame and are being asked how he was healed, then know this, you and all the people of Israel: It is by the name of Jesus Christ of Nazareth, whom you crucified but whom God raised from the dead, that this man stands before you healed. - Acts 4:8-10

And now, Lord, consider their threats, and enable Your servants to speak Your word with complete boldness, as You stretch out Your hand to heal and perform signs and wonders through the name of Your holy servant Jesus." After they had prayed, their meeting place was shaken, and they were all filled with the Holy Spirit and spoke the word of God boldly. - Acts 4:29-31

One day as we were going to the place of prayer, we were met by a slave girl with a spirit of divination, who earned a large income for her masters by fortune-telling. This girl followed Paul and the rest of us, shouting, "These men are servants of the Most High God, who are proclaiming to you the way of salvation." She continued this for many days. Eventually Paul grew so aggravated that he turned and said to the spirit, "In the name of Jesus Christ I command you to come out of her!" And the spirit left her at that very moment. - Acts 16:16-17

The Scripture leaves no room for doubt–great authority and power are unleashed when the name of Jesus is invoked. The early church saw it firsthand; they practiced it as they fulfilled their great commission. They wielded it in battle against the forces of darkness who tormented the people along their path.

What will be said about the modern church?

I am honestly embarrassed to admit I am guilty of the following...Relegating the most powerful name in the universe to a mere "yours truly" at the end of my prayers. Our modern, Western church has trained us that saying "in Jesus' name" is simply the proper "sincerely yours" sign-off to prayer.

Prayer, in Jesus' name, is infinitely more significant and powerful than the habitual closing of a letter or email. It entails approaching God on Jesus' merit, not our own. We now come to the throne room because Jesus' sacrificial death now allows us that privilege. Therefore, we can *approach God's throne of grace with confidence, so that we may receive mercy and find grace to help us in our time of need* (Hebrews 4:16) because we come in the name of, and by the sacrificial blood of our high priest–Jesus.

Because we are also now God's beloved children, we have full access to our Father. We are no longer slaves or orphans - but children, and joint heirs with Jesus. As children, we should be focused on praying for things that bring our Father glory and align our will and wishes with His. If that is our true motive, Jesus said , *whatever we ask in My name, that I will do, that the Father may be glorified in the Son.* - John 14:13

While these approaches to praying in Jesus' name are absolutely Biblical and correct, I am concerned that most Christians (self included) have simply formed a habit of asking God for things and adding the "in Jesus' name" tagline. No deep thought or appreciation for why we are allowed to do so, or to the primary intent to bring God glory in the answer.

What is even more concerning is the lack of knowledge and practice by Christians of the ultimate authority and significant power inherent in the invoking of the name of Jesus in warfare-related prayer.

As we read earlier in this Chapter…

In my name, you will drive out demons and lay hands on the sick
and they will recover
Demons submit to us in your name
In the name of Jesus, get up and walk
In the name of Jesus I command you to come out of her

These are not the standard prayers we learned in Sunday School. These are declarations to our mortal enemy that he must submit, stand down, set free and flee at the mere mention of the name of Jesus. We (you and I) have no power in ourselves, but, as His children (with associated authority as joint heirs) and ambassadors, we have been given the right to invoke His name when we come face to face with the enemy and his schemes.

Yes, pray every prayer in the mighty name of Jesus and for His sake and glory - but, never fail to speak the name above every name when confronted by evil.

[*As a word of advice - the name "Jesus" is the name God chose to give His Son. It is at the name of Jesus that every knee will bow and tongue confess. It is the name of Jesus that the early followers invoked when addressing demons and sickness.*

Point is - it is not the name or title "Lord" or "Christ" or "Savior" alone that carries the authority and power of God. We must be deliberate in our use of the actual name "Jesus" alone or in combination with Lord and Christ for it to have the intended effect in battle.]

Let's look back at our illustration of dealing with someone wrestling with fear and fearful, dreadful thoughts. While the following is not offered as "the" way to pray, my hope is you will see a stark contrast and will begin to develop a more powerful, authoritarian prayer vocabulary in the future.

Prayer 1 (typical, former prayer of mine)

Father, I lift up _____ to you and ask Lord that you calm her fears and take them away. Would you be with her Lord and comfort her during this time. Help her not be fearful and learn to trust You with whatever is going on right now in her life.

In Jesus' name - Amen

Prayer 2 (a different approach)

Thank You Father that because of the sacrifice on Jesus on my behalf, I can come into Your presence to ask for grace to help in this time of need. Thank you that your Word says that Your "perfect love casts out all fear". We know fear is not from You, and therefore we join together now in Your presence, and invoke Your power and authority to deal with this scheme of the enemy.

In the mighty name and authority of Jesus, I take authority over this spirit of fear and command you to leave _____ immediately.

You have no right or authority to torment _____, and by the authority of the name and blood of Jesus Christ, I resist you and command you to leave her now and do not return. According to God's Word, you must flee.

Holy Spirit, would you come now and manifest Your peace to _____ and allow her to feel the overwhelming peace of Christ that passes all understanding, and to find deep rest in her soul. Thank You that You have not given _____ a spirit of fear but of power, love and a sound mind. May she rest now in your "perfect love".

I ask all of this in the mighty name and authority of Your Son, Jesus. - Amen

---

Again, there is no absolute right or wrong way to pray in a situation like this. My thought though…. is which prayer would have the most immediate impact on the source of fear, and bring relief to the person seeking prayer?

Scripture says that the name of Jesus has the power to deliver us from evil, to give us salvation, to cause every knee to bow, and to grant us access to the Heavenly Father as we pray. This power we can't fully explain or comprehend, yet we have the right as children of God to invoke our Lord's powerful name. Not only do we have the right, but we have the responsibility as we minister in His name.

As God's children and followers, we have been given authority "over all the power of the evil one"(Luke 10:19), we have been given "divinely powerful weapons" (2 Corinthians 10:4) we can deploy to pull down enemy strongholds in peoples' lives, the indwelling Spirit and power of God, and the most powerful name in the universe by which every evil force must submit....

None of which have any affect however if we don't:

a) know we have them, and

b) use them effectively.

It doesn't matter whether you want to be in a spiritual battle,
you are in one.
The battle is between good and evil,
and you are the prize.
Charles Stanley

CHAPTER TEN

So, Now What?

Land The Plane...

God created Satan

Satan rebelled

Satan was kicked out of heaven along with 1/3 of the angels

God created Adam & Eve

God gave them dominion over the earth

Adam & Eve fell for Satan's lies/deceit and abdicated their dominion

Satan became the "god of this world"

Jesus took back dominion at his death and resurrection

Satan is still allowed to rule for a predetermined time

Jesus gave authority over Satan's rulership and schemes to His disciples and followers

Satan and his forces are working 24/7/365 to "kill, steal and destroy" those followers

The spiritual war is on - and the battles rage on every day

The primary battle ground is our mind

We have been given divinely powerful weapons with which to fight and win these battles

We must know them–we must use them.

That about sums it up. But the battles truly are relentless, and Satan is playing for keeps. His goal is to utterly destroy your witness, legacy, health, mind, joy, family, marriage, friendships, finances, etc.–every aspect of your life. But he cannot do any of these, unless you allow him.

Would you consider trying to catch fish using only a hook? Probably not. Too obvious, right? Why?

A plain, shiny silver hook doesn't resemble anything that is appealing to a fish. That's exactly why the aisles of fishing tackle at Bass Pro/Cabelas (and others) are filled with a fish-friendly smorgasbord of artificial frogs, worms, minnows, bugs, crawfish, spiders and more. Why?

Because these delicacies are what fish love to eat. And in order to get a fish to bite your sharp, shiny hook (and reel him into your boat), you have to deceive him into thinking he is biting into one of his favorite snacks.

An astute fisherman knows what fish like what snack. Then he/she throws said snack into the fish's habitat and works the "bait" to make it appear very life-like and appealing. If the fisherman is good at his deception, and the bait looks appealing enough–BAM–fishy takes a big bite assuming it will taste so delicious and satisfy his instinctive need for food.

Poor Fish.

He thought he was going to enjoy a delicacy–but ended up in a live well–with a very sore mouth–on his way ultimately to a hot fryer or mounted on a trophy wall.

I know–I was supposed to be landing the plane.

As you can tell, the point is this: Satan is a master fisherman, with untold years of experience. He is an expert, a master of the craft. He knows what "bait" to use on us, at the appropriate time and how to make it look as attractive as possible.

Remember the analogy of Eve and Jesus in Chapter 7, and how they approached their respective temptations?

We cannot keep Satan from throwing bait our way. We cannot stop the thoughts, the temptations or his relentless attempts…but, we have choices we can control (with God's help):

We hear a voice, a thought, that seems very attractive, very "reasonable" and justified–it doesn't look at all like a sharp, silvery hook or we would turn away. It is bait, right? It is supposed to look good...

An attractive co-worker, just one drink, a quick peek at an adult website or image, or those "real" thoughts of panic/despair that your situation is out of control–you name it–there are a million of them. And the "fisherman" makes them seem so realistic, so desirable, and right then ...in that moment...you have a choice to make.

Jesus said... No way... "the Bible says...this is what is true and I am not falling for your lies and deception–Be gone!" End of temptation–end of battle...for now.

Eve said..."Wow, this looks very tasty. I deserve this. Just a little bite won't hurt anything. Maybe God didn't say that. No one will know"...BAM–hook in mouth–reeled in...death.

> But each one is tempted
>> when by his own evil desires he is lured away and enticed.
>> Then after desire has conceived, it gives birth to sin;
>> and sin, when it is full-grown, gives birth to death.
> James 1:14-15

All of us are tempted. The question is - what do we do with that temptation? Temptation is normal, and temptation is not sin. Lures look amazingly real. They are intended to lure us away, and entice us. If we turn toward them, believe the lie and swim after them - we have made our choice....

The more we look, the more we ponder, the more we justify.... the tastier the bait appears. When our temptation lures us away from what we know is right (righteous) and we ponder (consider long enough to become enticed) - we allow desire to be conceived ... it becomes alive... and begins to grow inside our mind/will, until we have crossed the line from temptation to sin. Sin is then birthed in our heart/mind.

Then we allow that desire to grow from "birth" to "full-grown" …a real event happens, we give in (submit) to the temptation….and the hook has been set..BAM..we are hauled in, and deep fried. Our sin leads to our death. Spiritual death = separation from God…..or, possibly actual death at the hands of that full grown sin (think anorexia, alcoholism, drug addiction, suicide, etc.).

Let us never forget - our enemy's main objective, his 24/7/365 goal - is to "kill, steal and destroy" us.

Let's see this process in action…Solomon gives us a great illustration in **Proverbs, Chapter 7: 6-27.**

For at the window of my house I looked through the lattice. I saw among the simple, I noticed among the youths, a young man lacking judgment, crossing the street near her corner, strolling down the road to her house, at twilight, as the day was fading into the dark of the night.

Then a woman came out to meet him, with the attire of a harlot and cunning of heart. She is loud and defiant; her feet do not remain at home. Now in the street, now in the squares, she lurks at every corner. She seizes him and kisses him, she brazenly says to him: "I have made my peace offerings; today I have paid my vows. So I came out to meet you; I sought you, and I have found you. I have decked my bed with coverings, with colored linen from Egypt. I have perfumed my bed with myrrh, with aloes, and with cinnamon. Come, let us take our fill of love till morning. Let us delight in loving caresses! For my husband is not at home; he has gone on a long journey. He took with him a bag of money and will not return till the moon is full."

With her great persuasion she entices him; with her flattering lips she lures him. Suddenly he follows her, like an ox going to the slaughter, like a deer bounding into a trap, until an arrow pierces his liver, like a bird darting into a snare—not knowing it will cost him his life. Now, my sons, listen to me, and attend to the words of my mouth. Do not let your heart turn aside to her ways; do not stray into her paths. For she has brought many down to death; her slain are many in number. Her house is the road to Sheol, descending to the chambers of death.

Think with me through this story…

1. A young man, strolling down the road to the wayward woman's house in the early evening…..think this was an accident? I think he knew who she was and where she lived. Based on the first few verses, this fella may have seen her out on the streets previously, and been tempted to try his luck. How long had he pondered the idea? How long had he battled this scenario in his mind? Had he battled it at all?

2. He waits until evening, maybe so as not to be seen. He had obviously planned this potential encounter. She comes out to meet him, scantily clothed, and seduces him with her flattering, sensuous, tempting words. Her husband is gone on a long trip, and no one will ever know……

3. Think about the James 1 verse, and see if you can tell at what point this lad is *lured away and enticed by his own desires - when was that desire conceived - and given birth to sin; and how quickly sin became full-grown, and gave birth to death?* Can you see the progression?

Now, take a minute and think about a recent scenario of your own…see if you can follow the progression there too.

The bottom line is this–we will all be tempted. Note that after Jesus successfully triumphed over Satan's temptation in the wilderness, the Scripture tells us that Satan left him, "for a more opportune time". He didn't leave for good. He left, but stayed close by in order to try another lure at a more opportune time…meaning, he lost that battle, but he would try, try again. And - the same happens to us…every single day.

The key is this–will we think about what we are thinking about and catch those tempting thoughts early? Will we claim God's truth over the situation before us, and resist the lure–no matter how attractive?

God promises strength, power, weapons, armor, etc.–but it is up to us to take advantage of those and utilize them every day to win battle after battle. We are at war, and war is hard. Passivity and complacency are not options–they will be our undoing.

Remember the words of John Piper–

Until you know that life is war, you do not know what prayer is for.

Conclusion

⁓

Eat This, Not That! is popular diet book by David Zinczenko (formerly editor of Men's Health) and chef Matt Goulding. Throughout the book, they focus on taking in fewer calories than your body burns every day. You do that by choosing to "eat this" food, and "not that" one. Easy, right?

Ask anyone who has ever attempted a diet plan and they will tell you it is not. The sight and smell of delicious food, fattening as it may be, becomes even more attractive when compared to the salad on your plate. Eat cauliflower, not pasta. Eat arugula, not hamburger. Eat cottage cheese, not chocolate ice cream. I get angry just thinking about it.

But, to the point - if we want to be victorious in getting our body in shape, we must become more deliberate about choosing what we should eat instead of what we want to eat. Yes, it is hard, but success is sweet. When tempted to eat what we know we shouldn't, we must pause and think. Is it really worth it? How badly do I want the positive results? Where is this urge/voice/lure coming from?

The bottom line to victory…a series of choices. When the thoughts come flooding into my mind, I cannot afford to linger, to ponder, to make agreement with the voice in my head that says, "just one bite won't matter", "no one is watching", and "you've been doing so good, you deserve a little splurge". The lure looks so very appealing....

Not that losing weight or maintaining a healthy weight and lifestyle aren't important, but they pale in comparison to the life and death choices facing all believers every day. Instead of vegetables vs. pasta - many face choices like depression or hope, anxiety or peace, addiction or freedom, and trust or infidelity.

As we have discussed, the war, the daily battles, the lures, the voices - are relentlessly assaulting our mind. We must win control of our thoughts if we have any chance of remaining victorious. Now that you know where the voices come from, who the enemy really is, who you are, and what God has provided you as weapons to fight with...the choice, once again, is yours.

What will you do now?

What will you do tomorrow...the next day...the next....

Should I call this The Brain Diet?

Not sure, but the following are my attempt to simplify our "Eat This" list in order to achieve victory in our daily lives:

1. **Read.** Fill your mind with God's truth. It is not enough to simply "have a quiet time". We must approach God's Word with the intent of learning, of preparing, of suiting up for today's battles. We don't read for reading sake, but for equipping.

2. **"Renew your mind"** daily by reading deeply of God's Word. Romans 8 - *For those who are according to the flesh set their minds on the things of the flesh, but those who are according to the Spirit, the things of the Spirit. For the mind set on the flesh is death, but the mind set on the Spirit is life and peace, because the mind set on the flesh is hostile toward God*

   The truth of God Word will "set you free".... so the more of it you know, the freer you will live. Meditate on the verses that speak life to you.

Know who you are in Christ (later in this chapter). Believe it, receive it, walk in it.

Know what authority, weapons and power you can wield against the enemy when he assaults you...... then USE THEM.

3. **Pray.** Prayer is NOT simply asking God for stuff. He is not our genie in a lamp.

   Prayer is simply an ongoing conversation between a Father and son/daughter who love each other deeply.

   It is an amazing privilege and opportunity to spend our day with the most loving, caring, forgiving, kind, understanding, wise, accepting and powerful Father you could ever imagine.

   He deeply wants to be involved in every detail of our lives, if we will allow Him. - so why would we not take advantage of that?

   As a father of three amazing sons, it would break my heart to spend an entire day in the car with one of them and he never talk with me. God longs to talk with you too.

4. **Worship.** Fill your mind, your car and your home with worship/praise. The enemy hates it. Whether you can sing or not - let your heart and mouth be filled with thanksgiving and praise for Who God is, and what He has done, and will do, in your life.

5. **Resist.** God promised, *"if you resist the enemy, he **will** flee"* (James 4:7). So, when you are tempted, when you see/think about that attractive lure, do what Jesus did..... immediately resist. Speak the Word of God, take the thought captive, and tell the enemy (out loud) to flee from your presence and your thoughts. Then replace the tempting thought with truth, praise, thanksgiving, etc...do NOT ponder, consider or spend any time thinking about what the enemy is offering. If you do...you lose. Take thoughts captive.

6. **Unite.** If you continue to struggle with tempting thoughts, ask a close friend or family member, small group leader, pastor or elder to join with you, regularly, and pray. Do not be embarrassed…everyone is tempted. It's okay to ask for help… Fight side-by-side with other people and see what God will do. Remember - *"He who is in you is greater than he who is in the world".*

Try this…not that….

When a destructive, tempting thought confronts you–begin confessing aloud the following truths from God's Word–and resist. This, my friends is true. This–is who you are, and Whose you are….

Who I Am In Christ

I Am Accepted in Christ

John 1:12	I am a child of God
John 10:27-30	I am His sheep and He knows me personally
John 15:15	I am Christ's friend
John 15:16	He chose me and appointed me to bear fruit
Romans 5:1	I have been justified and sanctified in Christ
Romans 8:28-30	I am called according to His purpose
I Cor. 6:20	I have been bought with a price: I belong to God
I Cor. 8:3	I am known by God
I Cor. 12:27	I am a member of Christ's Body
Gal. 4:4-7	I am a child of God and also an heir
Eph. 1:1	I am a saint
Eph. 1:5	I have been adopted as God's child
Eph. 2:18	I have direct access to God through the Holy Spirit
Col. 1:14	I have been redeemed and forgiven of all my sins
Col. 2:10	I am complete in Christ

I Am Secure in Christ

Luke 10:18	My name is written in heaven
Romans 4:7-8	My sins have completely and permanently forgiven
Romans 5:1-2	I have peace with God

Romans 6:18	I have been set free from the law of sin
Romans 8:1,2	I am forever free from condemnation
Romans 8:28	I am assured that all things work together for my good
Romans 8:35	I cannot be separated from the love of God
I Cor. 1:7-9	I do not lack any spiritual gift
I Cor. 3:16	God's Spirit lives in me
2 Cor. 1:21	I have been established, anointed and sealed by God
2 Cor. 5:17	I am a brand new creation in Christ
Gal. 2:20	Christ lives in me
Gal. 5:1	Christ has set me free from Satan's bondage
Eph. 2:1-10	I am seated with Christ in heavenly places, far above Satan's dominion
Phil. 1:6	I am confident that god will perfect the good work He has begun in me
Phil. 3:20	I am a citizen of heaven
2 Tim. 1:7	I have not been given a spirit of fear, but of power, love and a sound mind
Heb. 4:16	I can always come before Him to find grace and mercy in time of need
I John 5;18	I am born of God and the evil one cannot touch me

I Have Authority in Christ

Luke 10:17-18	He has given me authority over all the power of the enemy, in Him
Romans 8:26-27	The Holy Spirit intercedes for me in accordance with God's will
2 Cor. 10:4-5	I fight with divinely powerful weapons
Eph. 2:1-10	I am seated with Christ in heavenly places, far above all of Satan's rule
Phil. 4:13	I can do all things through Christ who strengthens me
Col. 2:9-10	Christ is the head over all power and authority, in heaven and on earth
Col. 2:15	Jesus has disarmed Satan and all of his forces
I Peter 3:12	The Lord is attentive to my prayers
I John 2:20-27	I have an anointing from the Holy Spirit

| I John 4:4 | Greater is He Who is in me than he that is in the world |
| James 4:7 | If I resist the devil, he will flee from me |

My True Identity

Satan's Lie	God's Truth
I am a sinner, because I sometimes sin	I am a saint (one declared righteous by God) who sometimes sins
I get my identity from what I have done	I get my identity from what God has done for me
I get my identity from what people say about me	I get my identity from what God says about me
My behavior tells me what to believe about myself	My belief in who God says I am determines my behavior

It is critical that we know who God says we are, because one of the most prevalent tactics used by our enemy is "accusation". He is called "the accuser of the brethren" in Revelation 12:10. You have most likely experienced thoughts similar to these familiar ones:

- "you're ugly", "you're fat", you look hideous"

- "no one really cares", "no one loves me"

- "my spouse will never change", "I deserve better than this", "what's the use"

- "I can't do anything right", "I suck at everything", "what's the use trying", "I'm a failure"

- "my life is out of control"

- "God can't love someone like me", "I'm probably not even saved", "what a hypocrite"

The list of Satan's accusations (lies) is endless, and when they are launched at you at an "opportune time", they become even easier to agree with. That is the key - DO NOT make agreement with any of Satan's lies. Once you agree in your heart/mind, then you give birth to these lies becoming a reality in our life. Remember - "*as a man thinks in his heart (mind), so is he*". You will become what you agree with and confess you are.

That is why you MUST know what God says about you, and who you really are in His eyes. This is our truth, our confession - our reality. Walk in these truths and you will not fall for the lies and accusations sent to "*kill, steal and destroy*" your joy, your health, your confidence, your hope, your witness, your freedom, and even your life.

In addition to knowing who you are, and what God says about you–it is critical that you know how to pray, to speak aloud, when the enemy assails us. We cannot afford to fall back on weak, impotent prayers to combat this type of "hand-to-hand combat". We must learn to pray with power and authority, to speak God's truth with confidence and conviction–to demolish strongholds and watch the enemy scamper.

One technique that has helped me tremendously in my own life is the use of "crafted" prayers. These are simply prayers that have been written down, or "crafted" ahead of time, and read out loud when the accuser speaks. The first accusation he will hurl at you is that your crafted prayer is "canned", that it "doesn't have any power or effect" because you are reading it. Nothing could be further from the truth...remember who the father of lies is...

So, let me share a few crafted prayers that you can use to craft your own, personalized version from. Crafted prayers simply provide language, when (like me) you find yourself at a loss for words in a particular situation that needs prayer. They also help me stay focused on the task at hand (confronting the enemy) when I might become distracted otherwise, or let my mind wander.

So, when you are tempted, when you see/think about that attractive lure, do what Jesus did...immediately resist–

Take the thought captive (*2 Corinthians 10:5*),

speak the Word of God (*Matt. 4:4,7,10*),

and tell the enemy (out loud) to flee from your presence and your thoughts. (*Js 4:7*)

Then replace the tempting thought with truth, praise, thanksgiving, etc...

do NOT ponder, consider or spend any time thinking about what the enemy is offering.

If you do...you will lose.

Sample Crafted Prayers

Evil Thought #1 - *"You are a failure/loser; no one appreciates/likes you; you'll never measure up; you are worthless; life's just not worth living; everyone would be better off without you, etc."*

Crafted Prayer:

Father, thank You that You love me. You love me so much You sent Jesus to die for me. Jesus, thank You for enduring such pain and anguish on the cross in order to take the penalty for my sin and make my salvation and eternal destiny possible. Thank

You Father that, according to Your Word, I am your child, and beloved by You. Thank You that You have great plans for my life, and You think about me continually. Thank You that there is nothing I could ever do to make You love me less, or love me more than You already do. I declare that I as Your child, I am priceless, I am completely and dearly loved and accepted. I am more than a conqueror because Christ lives in me, and my life matters. You have called me to be a light in this dark world and to stand out, to represent You wherever I go. Fill me Father afresh with Your Spirit now and allow me to feel Your love.

I declare now that as God's child, I have been given authority over all the power of my enemy, and I resist any thought that I am (a failure, unloved......*whatever you are dealing with.....*), and command it to flee from my mind and from my presence in the mighty name of Jesus Christ. I resist any scheme of the enemy to torment me, accuse me or depress me and cast them away from me also in Jesus' name. By the truth and the power of Your Word - I declare that no weapon formed against me will prosper.

Thank You Father that I am loved, I am valuable to You and to others, I am free, and Your Spirit lives in me. Fill my mind with truth and allow me to hear Your voice more clearly than ever before as I walk with You today. In the mighty and matchless name of Jesus, I pray.

Evil Thought #2 - *Overwhelming fear and/or anxiety*

Crafted Prayer:

Father, thank You that Your Word tells me not to "worry about anything, but to make my request of You and that Your peace will keep my heart and mind in Christ Jesus". So I bring this situation to You now and ask that You would replace my anxiety with Your peace. You are bigger than anything that troubles me, and nothing is impossible for You.

I stand against any spirit of fear and anxiety that is coming against me, and demand that it leave my thoughts and my presence, now, in the powerful name of Jesus.

I declare that I have not been given a spirit of fear, but of power, of love and of a sound mind. Based on this truth, I resist and rebuke all fearful and anxious thoughts now and bring them under the blood of Jesus. In Jesus' name, the name above all names, I resist these thoughts and bring this situation to Your feet, Lord. I release this situation to You, and ask for Your peace to overshadow and cancel any plan and scheme of the enemy. I rest in Your love and Your sovereign plan for my life. In the mighty name of Jesus I pray.

Evil Thought #3 - *Sadness, Hopelessness, Depression*

Crafted Prayer:

Father, You know my heart. You know I have been _____. I know the enemy would have me spiral down into a dark pit of depression and despair, and ultimately destruction - but, by an act of my will, I turn to You, Father and cry out for help. I resist and rebuke all spirits of sadness, hopelessness, depression and despair in the name of Jesus and command that you leave my thoughts and my presence. I am a child of God, a beloved son/daughter, and deeply loved. I confess that I am not _____, and have hope in Jesus and in His sovereign plan for my life.

I choose to find my joy in the Lord, knowing that His joy is my strength. My hope is in Him, not my circumstances. God is for me and He will protect me, comfort me, rescue me and provide for all my needs through His riches in Christ. I cast my cares upon You, Lord and know that You are more than able to handle them. You are able to do accomplish far more than I can even ask or imagine Father, so I place my hope in You and Your plan. Help me keep my thoughts on You and Your Word today.

———————

These are brief examples of what a crafted prayer may look like. I encourage you to get with God and develop prayers, as He leads you, to address the temptations and assaults you face personally. They will morph over time, as your life and situations change, but simply amend them accordingly. Don't let the enemy discourage you or convince you that these kinds of prayers are not powerful enough, reverent enough or effective enough. Invoking the name of Jesus, and speaking God's truth out loud–will send the enemy packing. As we saw with Jesus' temptation in the wilderness, however, they will relentlessly return and keep trying to destroy you. That is why we too must remain relentless to 1) put on the armor we have been given (daily), and 2) wield the "weapons of our warfare" in battle - as we learn to walk in 3) the authority given to us by Christ "over all the power of the enemy".

They overcame him by the blood of the Lamb, and the word of their testimony. **Revelation 12:11**

Jesus did his part.

His blood disarmed the enemy, and covered our past, present and future sin.

When God looks at you, He sees Jesus' blood which has forever justified us before Him.

We have been adopted and accepted by a Father Who loves us lavishly and that will never change. We are His beloved children, and joint heirs with Christ of His kingdom. All that He has is ours. We are seated with Him in heavenly places, far above all rule, and power and dominion.

We have been given armor, mighty weapons and divine authority (as His children) over all the power of the enemy.

Now, the only power our enemy has over us is the power we allow him to have.

We must control the battlefield of our mind.

Our testimony is who God says we are…

Believe it. Profess it. Walk in it.

Live Victorious!

www.ingramcontent.com/pod-product-compliance
Lightning Source LLC
Chambersburg PA
CBHW081551040426

42448CB00016B/3285